THE KNOWLEDGE-BASED ORGANIZATION
Four Steps to Increasing Sales, Profits, and Market Share

James A. Alexander

Michael C. Lyons, Ph.D.

IRWIN
Professional Publishing

Chicago • Bogotá • Boston • Buenos Aires • Caracas
London • Madrid • Mexico City • Sydney • Toronto

Editor in chief:	Jeffery A. Krames
Marketing manager:	Tiffany Dykes
Project editor:	Denise Santor-Mitzit
Production supervisor:	Pat Frederickson
Designer:	Keith McPherson
Art Manager:	Kim Meriwether
Compositor:	Electronic Publishing Services, Inc.
Typeface:	11/13 Palatino
Printer	Book Press, Inc.

Library of Congress Cataloging-in-Publication Data

The knowledge-based organization: Four steps to increasing sales, profits, and market share / James A. Alexander, Michael C. Lyons.

    p.   cm.
    ISBN 0–7863–0353–0
    1. Selling. 2. Customer relations. 3. Customer service—Management. 4. Sales management. I. Lyons, Michael C. II. Title.
    HF5438.25.A435   1995
    658.8'12—dc20   94-24540

Printed in the United States of America
1 2 3 4 5 6 7 8 9 0 BP 1 0 9 8 7 6 5 4

Preface

This is not another book on customer service or selling tactics.

THE NEED

Top organizations are already making the difficult product transition from selling goods to selling service, yet this isn't enough. Service is rapidly becoming a commodity with the consequences of relentless pressure on margins.

Now in an effort to generate new, higher-margin revenue, leading-edge businesses are addressing a need that goes beyond selling service. They face the daunting task of selling *knowledge* as the product.

Harnessing knowledge demands a new model for doing business—the creation of the Professional Services organization. As Tom Peters states, "All firms are becoming Professional Services firms." Professional Services is the model for creating tomorrow's competitive organization.

Throughout this book the term *Professional Services* expands beyond its traditional usage of describing law, medical, design, and consulting firms. Professional Services is used to describe a strategy, a capability, and a mindset. It is just as applicable to an office furniture manufacturer as it is to a computer software company or a telecommunications business.

Professional Services is defined as "the systematic application of knowledge to improve performance." Knowledge is the product and the value is improved customer performance.

Successfully implementing Professional Services calls for the integration of sales and service capabilities. Until now there has not been a model or an action plan for transforming sales and service into the Professional Services organization.

TARGET AUDIENCE

This book is written for business executives tasked with the responsibility for improving the revenue (customer) side of the business: sales, service, and marketing. It will be of most value to organizations that sell and service in business-to-business environments undergoing rapid change.

THE PURPOSE

The purpose of this book is to help business leaders make the transformation to Professional Services. It draws from what we have learned through on-going international research and hands-on implementation consulting.

The book is meant to be used as an application guide. The focus is to stimulate thought, spur action, and provide a general road map of change and improvement. It is a starting point and an on-going reference for any business leader trying to differentiate his or her organization from the competition.

The book

- Explains why the existing sales and service strategies are no longer appropriate.
- Establishes the Professional Services model necessary to compete in the next century.
- Lays out the steps necessary to transition from the existing sales and service paradigms to the new Professional Services model.
- Explains common problems in implementing Professional Services and how to handle them.
- Shares real-world examples.
- Provides tools for use in your own organization.

HOW TO USE THIS BOOK

The book is divided into two parts. Part I provides the rationale for sales and service leaders to transition to Professional Services. It explains the main elements of the Professional Services model:

selecting the strategy, organizing the business, defining the processes, and establishing and managing the Professional Services team. Part I provides the reader with the conceptual framework and practical model of an up-and-running, high-performance Professional Services organization.

Part II is a step-by-step guide to accelerating the transition to Professional Services. It starts with a discussion of the transition and the need to manage it like a project. Part II then explains the four phases needed to effectively manage the Professional Services transition project: discovery, blueprinting, achievement, and tracking. Part II provides the reader with the how-to, nuts-and-bolts steps to effectively and efficiently manage the sales and service transition to Professional Services.

James A. Alexander
Michael C. Lyons, Ph.D.

Acknowledgements

As astute readers will recognize, this book is built on the preceding work of numerous authors. Especially influential are the writings of Peter Drucker, Thomas Gilbert, Geary Rummler, James Quinn, Mack Hanan, Michael Porter, and Tom Peters. Good stuff.

Strong influence comes from more personal experience. The broad integration and application of project management are attributed to Bob Brinkerhoff. The strong performance engineering focus and the critical thinking behind it have been impacted by Dale Brethower. Thank you both.

Joe Trpik provided the encouragement and the support of the Association for Services Management International to conduct much of our research with leading-edge companies. Thanks, Joe.

Two colleagues deserve special credit: Brian Scharp for building the relationship with Irwin and providing all the graphics and Carla Messer for the seemingly endless rounds of review and feedback. The book couldn't have been written without your outstanding support.

Contents

Part I
THE HIGH-PERFORMANCE PROFESSIONAL SERVICES ORGANIZATION   1

Chapter One
SELECTING THE STRATEGY   3

The Quandary, 3
Nobody's Satisfied, 4
A Question of Focus, 4
Customer Differences, 4
The Traditional Strategy, 7
The Value–Added Strategy, 9
The Professional Services Strategy, 10
Selecting the Strategy, 12

Chapter Two
ORGANIZING THE BUSINESS   16

A Brand New Business, 16
Functional Silos, 17
   The Typical Marketing Function, 17
   The Typical Sales Function, 18
   The Typical Service Function, 19
Cracks in the Concrete, 19
The Principles of Organizing, 20
   Fluid Information, 20
   Focused Power, 21
   Flexible Structure, 22
   Fundamental Values, 23
Organizing around Processes, 25

Chapter Three
DEFINING THE PROCESS   27

The Four Core Professional Services Processes, 27
The Marketing Process, 27
The Qualifying Process, 32
The Selling Process, 34
   Relationship Manager, 36
   Account Team, 37
   Account Objectives, 39
   Opportunities, 39
   Risks, 39
   Considerations, 39
   Stakeholder Analysis, 39
   Critical Events, 40
   Action Steps, 40
The Consulting Process, 41
Special Challenges of Professional Services
Processes, 42

Chapter Four
BUILDING THE HIGH-PERFORMANCE
PROFESSIONAL SERVICE TEAM   44

The Good Old Days of Service, 44
The Good Old Days of Selling, 45
The Big Leap, 46
The Four Critical Capabilites, 47
   Selling Skills, 47
   Project Management, 48
   Technical Knowledge, 48
   Business Acumen, 49
Hire, Train, or Outsource, 49
The Performance System, 49
   Create Clear Performance Specifications, 50
   Determine Logical Work Flow, 52
   Provide Adequate Resources, 52
   Establish Consequences, 53

Provide Feedback, 53
Recognize and Reward, 54

Part II
ACCELERATING IMPLEMENTATION   57

Chapter Five
MANAGING THE TRANSITION   59

There's No Place Like Home, 59
Horror Stories, 60
The Transition Force Field Analysis, 61
  Senior Management Commitment, 62
  Team Buy In, 64
  Customer Value, 65
  Leadership, 65
  Adequate Resources, 66
The Professional Services Transition
Project, 67
The Transition Project Team, 68
Managing the Transition, 69

Chapter Six
PHASE 1: DISCOVERY   72

The Problem with Traditional Market Research, 73
Amplify the Voice of the Customer, 74
Voice of the Customer Example, 78
Assessing Business Issues, 81
Business Issues Example, 83

Chapter Seven
PHASE 2: BLUEPRINTING   85

Blueprinting Rationale, 85
Blueprinting Session Guidelines, 87
  Prepare Senior Management, 87
  Use Outside Facilitators, 88

Allow Enough Time, 88

Get Away, 88

Plan Carefully, 88

Be Flexible, 89

The Blueprint, 89

Fundamental Values: The Organization's Conscience that Creates a Touchstone for Decision Making, 90

Vision: A Vivid Picture of Where the Organization Must Go, What It Must Become, and How It Will Get There, 90

Goals: Clear, Achievable, Measurable, and Motivational PS Priorities, 91

Focus: Identification of the Core Competency, High-Priority Customers, Markets, and Products, 91

Blueprint Benefits, 93

Stakeholder Buy In, 93

Recruitment and Selection Tool, 93

Account Qualification, 93

Marketing Tool, 94

Financial Return, 94

Transition Project Plan, 94

Project Definition, 95

Objectives, 95

Stakeholder Analysis, 95

Force Field Analysis, 96

Critical Tasks, 96

Develop People, 97

Chapter Eight
PHASE 3: ACHIEVEMENT   99

Develop Processes, 100

Effective Processes, 100

Customer Value, 100

Performance Goals, 100

Clearly Understood Procedures, 101

Ownership, 101

Simplicity, 101

Develop Process Action Steps, 101
Develop Products, 108
    Training, 109
    Process Reengineering, 110
    Outsourcing, 110
Professional Services Pricing Issues, 110
Pricing Maxims, 111
Pricing Strategies, 112
    Time and Materials, 112
    Project, 112
    Pay for Performance, 113
Product Design, 113
Develop People, 114
    Analyze Star Performers, 115
High-Impact Training, 119
Continuous Learning, 120

Chapter Nine
PHASE 4: TRACKING   122

Manage Relationships, 123
Manage Risks and Opportunities, 127
Day-to-Day Tracking, 129
Conclusion, 130

Illustrations

Figure 1–1. Customer Expectation Hierarchy

Figure 1–2. The Three Sales and Service Strategies

Figure 2–1. The Three Silos

Figure 2–2. Process

Figure 3–1. The Four Core Professional Services Processes

Figure 3–2. Marketing Professional Services

Figure 3–3. Qualifying Professional Services

Figure 3–4. Key Success Factors

Figure 3–5. Selling Professional Services

Figure 3–6. Key Account Planner

Figure 3–7. Consulting Professional Services

Figure 4–1. The Four Critical Capabilities

Figure 4–2. Professional Services Performance System

Figure 4–3. Professional Services Performance Checklist

Figure 5–1. Professional Services Transition Force Field Analysis

Figure 5–2. Professional Services Transition Project

Figure 5–3. Managing the Transition: The Four Phases

Figure 6–1. Traditional Market Research versus Discovery Research

Figure 6–2. Amplify the Voice of the Customer

Figure 6–3. Assess Business Issues

Figure 7–1. Blueprint Example

Figure 7–2. Professional Services Transition Project Plan

Figure 8–1. The Ideal Qualifying Process

Figure 8–2. The Existing Qualifying Process

Figure 8–3. The New Qualifying Process

Figure 8–4. Developing Products

Figure 8–5. Steps to Product Design

Figure 8–6. Professional Services Competency Profile
Figure 8–7. High-Impact Training
Figure 9–1. Manage Relationships and Manage Risks
        and Opportunities
Figure 9–2. Stakeholder Analysis
Figure 9–3. Contingency Plan

I

THE HIGH -
PERFORMANCE
PROFESSIONAL
SERVICES
ORGANIZATION

B efore creating the Professional Services organization, it is important to understand the rationale on which the organization is built. Part I explains the strong need for major changes in sales and service and then reviews the available options. The case is made that Professional Services is the mandate for the future.

Part I describes all the critical elements of the Professional Services system. It provides a working model of the high-performance Professional Services organization based on both solid theory and hands-on experience.

Chapter One

Selecting the Strategy

The Quandary

Nobody's Satisfied

A Question of Focus

Customer Differences

The Traditional Strategy

The Value-Added Strategy

The Professional Services Strategy

Selecting the Strategy

THE QUANDARY

Sales and service executives are in a quandary. They are *asked* to lower prices while maintaining margin and are *told* to generate new revenue while cutting budgets. In response, sales and service managers scratch their heads, roll up their sleeves and exhort their people to "do more with less."

The typical sales manager's rallying cry is "sell more, better, harder, faster. Feet to the street. Two more calls a day. Watch your phone bill and back off on entertainment."

Service managers direct their personnel to "reduce comebacks, make more service calls, and complete them more quickly. Sell more maintenance contracts and manage your inventory. Plan your day more efficiently and bill a higher percentage of your service call time. Sorry we cut your administrative support."

Finally, territories are reorganized, compensation plans are changed, and field managers are axed in an effort to make things happen.

NOBODY'S SATISFIED

When the dust settles, the results are predictable—minimal improvement in the numbers and a small return from the vast output of resources and effort. Executives are disgruntled at the lack of results. They rush to develop a new promotional campaign, investigate better automation, create a different incentive program, or make further cuts.

Field personnel are weary from the added pressure and the longer hours. They are disenchanted with the meager results gained from the addition of brute effort. They have confirmed what they already knew—**doing more of the same activities yields more of the same results.**

A QUESTION OF FOCUS

A major contributor to this activity trap is a lack of focus. Most sales and service organizations try to be all things to all customers. Every customer is seen as being a good customer. The quality of customers is determined by how quickly they pay their invoice. Any customer that pays within 60 days is solid.

Sales personnel are provided with the same training, the same brochures, and the same incentives for working with vastly different customers. A sale is a sale. Never mind business fit, strategic value, or the true cost of sale.

Service personnel provide the same offering, the same way for all customers. The service standards are the same for the large, complex national account as they are for the mom and pop down the road. One size fits all.

This lack of focus comes from failing to *systematically* address customer differences.

CUSTOMER DIFFERENCES

For every $5 that the traditional marketing function spends analyzing customers' needs around the product, only $1 is spent analyzing customer needs for servicing/application of that product.[1]

---

[1] Quinn, J B (1992). *Intelligent enterprise: A knowledge and service based paradigm for industry.* New York: Free Press.

FIGURE 1–1
Customer Expectation Hierarchy

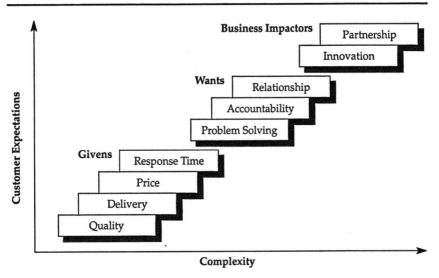

Newly created services marketing departments mimic this pattern and focus on product mix and pricing rather than understanding and meeting evolving customer expectations. While customers are being taken for granted, their loyalty is eroding.

Getting the field organization back on track begins by understanding and systematically addressing customer similarities and differences. Our customer expectation research shows that an organization's customers cluster into three categories. The customers in one category have key expectations that are distinct from the expectations in the other two categories. Each customer is unique; however, certain types of customers share certain sets of expectations about the suppliers they deal with. Figure 1–1 demonstrates the different categories of customers and how the expectations of these customers form a hierarchy.[2]

---

[2] Our research demonstrates that all customer expectations cluster into three major expectation categories. The specific expectations within those categories and the definition of those expectations such as *problem solving, accountability,* and so on will vary among industries. Figure 1–1 is an example from a specific customer. It is not meant to be representative of all customers or all industries.

Customers from the first category, givens, expect just the basics. This group wants quality products delivered on time at the lowest possible cost. They expect service when they call, and they don't expect to pay for it.

Customers in the second category, wants, assume the basics and want more. This group looks to suppliers to help them maximize their product investment. They expect troubleshooting and want suppliers to offer ideas and better ways of doing things.

Customers in the third category, business impactors, assume all the expectations of the first two categories and want an even higher level of satisfaction. Customers from this select group really mean it when they say they want a partnership or business alliance. In addition, when they perceive the value, they are willing to pay for it.[3]

The customer hierarchy allows the supplier organization to stratify its customers into three basic groups, each with distinct expectations. Segmenting customers into categories is important because it forces the supplier organization to address two of its biggest problems—resource allocation and realistic pricing. Segmenting customers allows the supplier organization to logically, systematically, and efficiently allocate the minimum amount of resources needed to meet the distinct expectations of the different customer categories at the highest price.[4]

For each category of the customer expectation hierarchy, there is a discrete strategy that focuses on meeting or exceeding the expectations for the customers in that category. The three strategies include traditional, value added, and Professional Services. Sales and service organizations must choose one and implement changes based on that strategy.[5] Figure 1–2 outlines and compares the core elements of each sales and service strategy.

---

[3] Our service quality research, this category showed the biggest gap between expectation and perceived satisfaction.

[4] Allocating resources by customer expectation category should impact many aspects of the organization including structure, roles and responsibilities, and performance objectives.

[5] Porter, M E (1980). *Competitive strategy: Techniques for analyzing industries and competitors.* New York: Free Press. Porter states that an organization can successfully implement only one major strategy. Mixed strategies are not effective. This brings up an interesting dilemma for sales and service organizations transitioning from one strategy to another. They must decide whether to have the entire organization adapt one strategy or create a separate organization with its own distinct strategy.

FIGURE 1–2
The Three Sales and Service Strategies

	Traditional	Value-Added	Professional Services
Customer Category	Givens	Wants	Business Impactors
Product	Goods	Service	Knowledge
Relationship	Vendor	Select supplier	Partner
Goal	Maintain Product	Improve application	Improve business
Performance measure	Efficiency	Effectiveness	Innovation

THE TRADITIONAL STRATEGY

The traditional strategy is most appropriate in dealing with customers in the givens category. The product the givens customer is most interested in is the tangible goods, "the box." Physical product characteristics are key purchase determinants as the customer considers and compares specifications, tolerances, and robustness of design.

No matter what their advertising states or what their annual report proclaims, givens customers think of suppliers as vendors and will choose any vendor that can responsively deliver adequate quality at the lowest possible price. To this group, vendors are vendors. By definition, vendors are easily replaced.

The goal of the traditional strategy is to maintain that physical product. Sell the product and provide just enough service to keep the product working and the competition out. Long-term, high-volume contracts should be an on-going objective.

Performance measures of the traditional strategy are centered around efficiency. Sales performance measures include sales per sales representative, close ratio, sales calls per day, volume per sales order, and sales volume compared to sales expense.

In the traditional strategy, since service is "free," service is seen as a cost center. Service performance measures are mainly geared toward lowered cost. The most common performance measures include warranty cost and service expense in relation to sales volume.

To maximize efficiency, service should focus on remote diagnostics and phone fixes. On-site visits should be a last resort. Ideally, the product is sold with the customer assuming the main servicing responsibility. This is critical since the customer won't pay for service anyway. Manuals with clear, detailed information should be provided to the customers to encourage them to assume maintenance responsibilities.

In the traditional strategy, if the product and the price are right, the more sales calls made, the more business sold. Therefore, sales representatives must maximize the hours of actual selling time and focus on the largest volume potential accounts. Whenever possible, the fax and phone should replace the face-to-face visit.

Efficiency is critical, and this traditional strategy demands continually looking for alternative ways to meet minimum sales/service requirements at less expense. When implementing this strategy, questions to ask include these: What is the minimum amount of resources we can expend to maintain our product? Do we need to send out service personnel or can the situation be handled over the phone? Do we need to have our own service people or can we outsource? Are separate service people needed at all—can our sales/service needs be handled with one customer contact person? Do we even need field people? Can sales objectives be met through telemarketing? Can telemarketing be outsourced?

With this classification of customer, any dollar spent above and beyond this maintenance level is wasted. Givens customers see products as commodities, and price is the major purchase determinant. Relationships are not important to them because vendors are easily replaced.

Sales and service should constantly be asking manufacturing to provide low-cost, zero-defect products. Support groups should be asked to ignore the fancy brochures, ads, and promotional videos and concentrate on straight forward product fact sheets and clear, comprehensive service maintenance manuals for customer personnel. Efficiency must be the mantra throughout the organization.

Givens customers, who readily admit who they are, are straightforward to deal with: provide them with a product up to specs, at reasonable delivery, and at a continually lower price. They prefer a no-frills, no-nonsense approach. Negotiate a contract, fulfill your commitments, give them no hassles, see them in a year.

The problem arises, though, when givens customers masquerade as wants or even business impactor customers. It is fashionable among well-read customers to talk about forming partnerships and creating supplier-customer strategic alliances. Many givens customers talk the talk of partnership but are not prepared to walk the talk. Suppliers' waste and frustration grow as they try to meet the surface needs of givens customers who are talking about more than they will pay for. Sorting out the real givens customers from the impostors is a critical task and will be discussed in more detail later in the chapter.

THE VALUE-ADDED STRATEGY

The value-added strategy is most appropriate in dealing with customers in the wants category. Wants customers assume that the tangible goods from all top suppliers are adequate—"boxes are boxes, networks are networks" is their motto. What they are most interested in is service—the intangible support that surrounds the tangible goods.[6]

The type of relationship most appropriate in the value-added strategy is that of select supplier. Customers consciously look for a small number of suppliers that meet prescribed criteria. They value the supplier relationship and know that part of their satisfaction depends on it.

The goal of this strategy is to improve the application of the tangible goods. Suppliers try to satisfy customers by adding value through service.

The critical performance measures of the value-added strategy are centered around effectiveness. Depending on the industry, sales performance measures might include account penetration, account retention, profitability per account, profitability per salesperson, select industry market penetration, and customer satisfaction. Potential service performance measures include percentage of callbacks, service contracts sold/number of total customers, and customer evaluation of service quality.

---

[6] A common, simple definition of *service* has eluded authors. In his book *Service management and marketing: Managing the moments of truth in service competition* (1990. Lexington, MA: Lexington Books), Christian Gronroos offers 12 different definitions. Our favorite is one by Gummesson: "Service is something which can be bought and sold but which you cannot drop on your foot."

Wants customers understand the importance of personal relationships and expect someone to take responsibility for their satisfaction. They respect and value suppliers that can solve their application problems. Importantly, these customers are willing to pay for it.

All customer contact personnel delivering this strategy need a combination of technical and interpersonal skills to be effective. Since customers often don't readily see the added value the supplier provides, selling competence is vital to make this strategy succeed. This strategy positions the service function as a profit contributor; therefore, service must play its role in actively selling the added value.

Many executives find the "parts is parts" mentality of the wants customer a difficult pill to swallow. Their history may have centered around designing, building, marketing, and selling the latest technology. However, research has shown time after time that customers assume that any of the boxes would be adequate. They care about the box only if it does not work in the application for which it was sold.

When implementing the value-added strategy, the following questions need to be asked: What makes our services different and better? How does that add value to our customer's application? How can we quantify that value? What is our customer's perception of the value we add? How do they perceive how we compare with the competition? How can we better explain (sell) that value to the customer? What other services could we provide that the customer would pay for? What other services would they pay the most for?

THE PROFESSIONAL SERVICES STRATEGY

Professional Services is the third strategy. Professional Services is "the systematic application of knowledge to improve performance."[7] The Professional Services strategy is appropriate when dealing with business impactor customers; customers from complex, sophisticated organizations that have the potential to see

---

[7] Our definition.

and pay for the knowledge-based solutions Professional Services can offer.

Knowledge is the product of the Professional Service organization. It is usable information; expertise based on theory and proven models, gained from experiences of past failure and past success that can bring about positive change. The knowledge of Professional Services can be packaged in many different forms. The three broad knowledge product categories include training, process reengineering, and outsourcing. Professional Services products are discussed in more detail in Chapter Eight.

The relationship that business impactor customers seek is that of a partner—a compatible organization they can work with to achieve mutual success. For example, business impactor customers are willing to invest in new joint ventures, but they expect their supplier-partners to do the same thing.

The goal of the Professional Services strategy is to improve the customer's business performance. This is a significantly more ambitious goal than that of the value-added strategy. The Professional Services strategy focuses on positively impacting one or more of the customer's critical business issues. These are the issues that directly link to the competitiveness, profitability, and long-term future of the specific customer.

Performance measures center on the development of innovative solutions. Professional Services targets the critical business issues of the customer. In all probability, the customers have already spent their own time and resources trying to solve these problems. They have already exhausted all of the "easy fixes" and have proven that they don't work or don't work well enough. They are under the gun to make something happen.

This implies that the supplier organization should maintain the effectiveness performance measures of the value-added strategy, as well as include indicators tracking the amount of innovation delivered to the customer. Innovation measures come directly from the customer. These innovation measures might include the percentage of customer cycle time reduction for a key process, reduced system down time, and increased customer revenue per service technician.

The critical capabilities of Professional Services personnel are selling skills, project management, technical knowledge, and business acumen. The degree of expertise needed to deliver Professional Services is seldom resident in one or even two individuals. Chapter Four discusses the Professional Services team and reviews the critical capabilities in detail.

Business impactor customers probably account for only 5 to 25 percent of the accounts within an industry. Yet most often they are large, complex organizations that are the leaders within the industry. Solving their problems has the potential for the most profitability. In addition, lessons learned while partnering with this elite group can later be profitably applied to other customers that follow in the footsteps of the leaders.

Questions to ask when implementing the Professional Services strategy include these: What expertise do we have that our customers don't have and need? How can we position that expertise with key customer decision makers? What additional resources or systems must we add to deliver innovation to business impactor customers?

SELECTING THE STRATEGY

There are three steps to determining which strategy is right for your sales and service organization: categorize existing customers, analyze performance data, and confirm the business focus.

1. *Categorize existing customers.* First categorize your existing customers into givens, wants, and business impactors. Quantitatively based market research can be helpful in giving you an idea of classification, but this won't be enough. In fact, used alone, most quantitative techniques popular with traditional market research actually add to the problem. A report three inches thick summarizing a paper and pencil survey supported by detailed statistical analysis, charts, and graphs can give executives a very false sense of knowing their customers. Nor do customer satisfaction scores solve this problem. They are at too high a level and don't delve deeply enough into the meanings behind the scores.

It takes solid qualitative research methods such as focus groups and individual interviews with a cross-section of customers and customer personnel to truly understand customer expectations.

These qualitative research techniques are a part of the discovery process outlined in detail in Chapter Six.

Once the information is collected, sorting techniques[8] are used to segment customers into one of the three categories. Most organizations find that they are trying to meet the expectations of customers in the same way across all three categories.[9] Close analysis shows that organizational resources are often not being utilized in the most productive way.

2. *Analyze performance data.* Next, you should analyze performance data on representative customer samples from each category. Take a look at how much you have "invested" in certain customers as compared with the financial return you received. How much time was actually spent selling and servicing this account? By whom? How long was the selling cycle? Besides people's time, what other costs were incurred?

With which of these customers do you enjoy working? Which customers seem to enjoy working with you? If you had your choice, on which category of customers would you prefer to focus? Which customers will take you into the future?

Prepare to determine which 20 % of your customers yield 80 % of your business. Determine which category seems to be the best match between customer expectations and your existing and potential capabilities.

Too many sales and service organizations fall into the trap of providing nonvalue-added services. The solution to differentiating yourself in the marketplace isn't providing the "most" services. Rather, it is aligning the right solutions with customer expectations. Whether and how much the customer pays is the key to knowing whether services add value or not.

---

[8] The affinity process is a sorting technique used widely in quality function deployment (QFD). It is an interactive approach used to define and categorize expectations by capturing actual customer language. See S. Mizuno, (1988). *Management for quality improvement: The seven new QC tools.* Cambridge, MA: Productivity Press.

[9] For years sales organizations have created specialized selling roles, such as industry specialists and national account representatives, in an effort to meet different customer needs. The results of this specialization have been mixed. Though the individual salesperson's role has changed, neither the organization strategy nor the support system behind the salesperson has shifted dramatically enough to maximize the full improvement potential.

Review the services provided for the customer category you selected. Note which ones add no value to this group of customers. Calculate what the cost is. Also note which services the customers value but for which you are currently not being paid. This analysis will provide you with some rough benchmarks to demonstrate the potential for Professional Services.

A Professional Services strategy isn't a good solution for all your existing customer needs. As you define your strategy, some of your service products may have to be drastically changed or eliminated, and some of your existing customers might have to be "fired" and no longer pursued.

3. *Confirm the business focus.* Finally, as you consider the shift to a Professional Services strategy, confirm the business focus of your company. Make sure that you have a crystal clear idea of your chief executive's business focus and the role that he or she sees sales and service playing. There is no sense pursuing Professional Services if senior management still feels that building a better box is the key to success.

For most executives, Professional Services is a difficult concept to understand. They were brought up under the rules of a different game. When the Professional Services strategy is selected, senior management must be educated and sold on the power of Professional Services to increase profits, market share, and revenue. Chapter Seven addresses how to build a comprehensive, motivational strategy to propel the Professional Services organization.

To be competitive, every sales and service organization must choose one and only one strategy. It must focus energy and resources to make that strategy a reality.

If you align with the traditional strategy—stop reading right here—this isn't the best use of your time.

If you align with the value-added strategy—skim through the book to find specific information that is relevant to your situation.

If you choose the Professional Services strategy—Read on. The business impactor customer offers the greatest potential for increased revenue, improved margin, and opportunities to innovate and have fun. The following chapters will outline the steps to help you successfully transform sales and service into a high-performance Professional Services organization.

Chapter Two explains why the old approaches to organizational design are too narrow and inappropriate for Professional Services. It outlines the organizing principles necessary for a high-performance Professional Services organization.

Chapter Two

Organizing the Business

A Brand New Business
Functional Silos
Cracks in the Concrete
The Principles of Organizing
Organizing Around Processes

A BRAND NEW BUSINESS

Glad to have you with us. From here, the book will concentrate on putting the Professional Services strategy into action. Just because you have decided to offer Professional Services, don't produce any four-color brochures touting your new offering just yet. Professional Services is not for the faint of heart. There are many decisions to make and much work to be done.

Professional Services is a brand new business—a radically different business than the ones that most sales and service executives are used to. Remember that past success in implementing traditional or value-added strategies may work against successfully implementing the Professional Services strategy. It is important to start with a blank sheet of paper and an open mind. The only question is: What is the best way to deliver on the Professional Services strategy?

This chapter discusses creating the Professional Services business based on a set of organizing principles. We will begin by learning from past experience. We will first address the current status and challenges of the three functions of marketing, sales, and service. Next, we will talk about the principles of organizing a true Professional Services system. Then we will discuss organizing around processes.

FUNCTIONAL SILOS

Much has been written about the functional silos that exist inside the organization between research and development (R & D), marketing, manufacturing, design, and so on.[1] As you intuitively have guessed or know through experience, the same silo walls exist within the customer contact side of the business.

Anyone who has ever walked through the marketing department, strolled through sales, and then wandered downstairs to service immediately senses the difference. Marketing, sales, and service people look different, act differently, and even dress differently. They have their own cultures based on different underlying assumptions of how the world operates.[2] Functional silos contribute to these differences and the suspicion and distrust that result.

Figure 2–1 shows the three silos typical of most customer contact organizations. The typical focus, critical tasks, and viewpoints of these three functions are radically different.

The Typical Marketing Function

The focus of the typical marketing function is to deliver acceptable margins on all products. When it comes down to it, profitability across product lines and across individual products is the main driver of marketing.

Marketers are tasked with implementing the classic four Ps: product, price, place, and promotion.[3] They manage existing product life cycles and coordinate new product development with the inside of the organization (design, R&D, manufacturing, etc.). They follow the time-honored pricing formula of

Price = Cost + Margin desired by executive management – What sales argues is necessary to meet the competition + The amount needed to meet the margin objectives of the respective product manager

---

1 Rummler, G A, and A P Brache (1991). *Improving performance: How to manage the white space on the organizational chart.* San Francisco: Jossey-Bass.

2 Schein, E (1985). *Organizational culture and leadership.* San Francisco: Jossey-Bass.

3 McCarthy, E J, and A Brogowicz (1984). *Basic marketing: A managerial approach.* 8th ed. Homewood, IL: Richard D Irwin.

FIGURE 2–1
The Three Silos

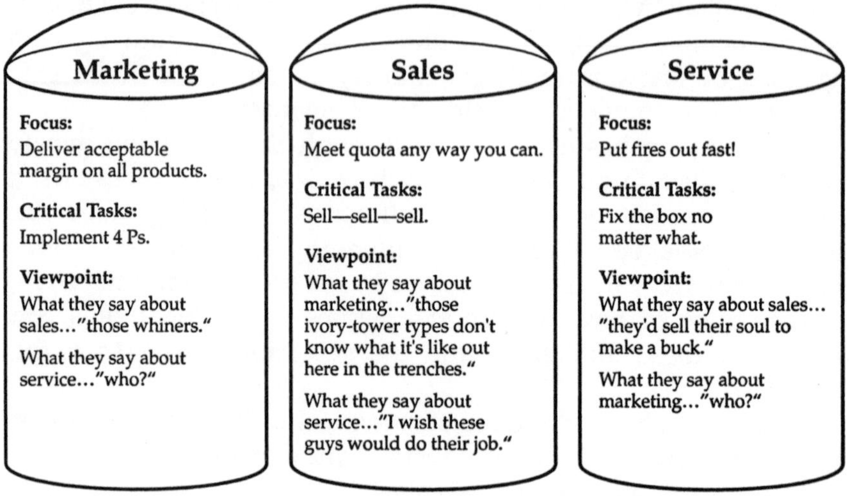

Marketing sizes the industry, segments the market, and does competitive analysis. It creates advertising, direct mail, sales support materials, and public relations campaigns. Newly created services marketing departments, although underfunded and understaffed, follow the same basic approach as their product marketing peers.

When asked their viewpoint about their colleagues in sales, marketers will smirk and respond, "Those whiners. They complain about everything. It's marketing that drives the company, you know." When asked about service personnel, they quizzically stare and ask, "Who?"

The Typical Sales Function

Compared to marketing, the typical sales silo is a less complex environment. The sales focus is to meet quota anyway possible. Sales wants to sell as much as it can to everyone who will pay close to on time, and without too much hassle. Its critical tasks are sell-sell-sell, uncover needs, introduce features and benefits, handle objections, close the order.

Ask a typical salesperson about marketing and you will get a 30-minute response starting out with a slow horizontal head shake and something like, "Those ivory tower types just don't understand what it is really like down here in the trenches slugging it out day after day. They spend all their time going to meetings and hiring consultants. If only they'd listen to us and put out the products we tell them to, we could dominate the market. It's sales that drives the company, you know."

The typical sales response to a question about service is "I wish those guys would do their job. You don't know how many times the customer calls me because service doesn't fix the problem. They must need more training. When I have to take my valuable time to talk to customers about old business, I'm not out there making new sales. It's sales that drives the company, you know."

The Typical Service Function

The service silo is simpler still. Its focus is to put out fires fast, make the product work no matter what it takes or what it costs. If you can't delight the customers, satisfy them. If you can't satisfy the customers, at least keep them from grumbling. There is only one critical task in the service silo and that is to fix the box and take the heat off of sales and the rest of the organization.

When asked about sales, service people grimly smile and say, "Well, you know how the 'suits' are. I think they'd sell their soul to make a buck. Eighty percent of the fires out here are started because sales oversold the product or sold it wrong. It's service that drives the company, you know."

When service personnel are asked about marketing, they quizzically stare and ask "Who?"

CRACKS IN THE CONCRETE

The analysis of the three silos is simple: conflicting focus, divergent critical tasks, and viewpoints that are often worlds apart. In addition, the thick walls created by an often competing functional management make communication among functions challenging and true cross-functional cooperation doubtful. Inevitably, the customer loses with a resulting flurry of finger pointing and cursing from one silo to another.

With the huge challenges facing marketing, sales, and service in implementing Professional Services, these silos can no longer be tolerated. A new way to organize must be found. Following the principles of organizing tears down silo walls and allows the Professional Services organization to dramatically increase its performance potential.

THE PRINCIPLES OF ORGANIZING

The Professional Services strategy calls for a more radical way of organizing the business. There are four Professional Services principles of organizing: fluid information, focused power, flexible structure, and fundamental values. The high-performance Professional Services organization lives by all four of these principles.

Fluid Information

Information is the raw material of Professional Services. Value-adding activity takes information and transforms it into knowledge, the product of Professional Services. Rich, in-depth information fuels the custom solutions required to meet the expectations of the complex customers of Professional Services. The information needed to implement these decisions may reside anywhere inside or outside the company.

In the past, the structure of the organization was the main vehicle for moving information around. Hierarchy and management controls were established to coordinate information flow. Worker, supervisor, manager, and executive each had a specific role in the transfer of information.

Information technology blasts away the need for traditional structures. Shared data bases, expert systems, and decision-support tools enable the organization to utilize information in ways unheard of just a few years ago. Organizations must rethink the whole usage of information and the systems needed to support it.

To be most valuable, information must be fluid—instantly available to all personnel for customer application at any time. If you can access *on site* everything from past sales call activity to customer financial data, you have a marked advantage over the competitor who cannot.

Therefore, the quality and speed of information directly impact performance and the resulting level of customer satisfaction. The Professional Services organization that has the most, best, and fastest information has a competitive advantage. With the new possibilities created by the latest in information technology, it is shortsighted not to aim for instant access to all organizational information.

For the Professional Services organization to meet the needs of current customers and to learn from its experiences to meet the expectations of future customers, information flow must be documented. Documentation of information flow is critical to the management of customer expectations. For example, when a customer problem arises, the logs of customer and internal interactions should be readily available to anyone in the Professional Services organization. This log of conversations and meetings should provide an audit trail in which to determine the root cause of problems as well as contributing factors.

Documentation also provides a history of innovation that can be applied to different situations with different customers. When innovative projects are completed, other people in the organization can readily access the critical information to speed learning and application to other situations. The documentation of followed practices and procedures simplifies problem analysis, speeds customer responsiveness, spreads innovation, and results in improved performance.[4]

The goal of fluid information is to have all of the right information available, all of the time, everywhere, to everybody.

Focused Power

Power is the capacity to mobilize people and resources to get things done.[5] Power can be granted and can be assumed. In Professional Services it takes power to commit to unusual customer requests, to propose untried solutions, and to negotiate complex contract terms.

---

[4] Many readers will observe that information documentation is at the heart of the ISO 9000 philosophy. These same quality concepts apply to Professional Services.

[5] Kanter, R M (1983). *The change masters*. New York: Simon & Schuster.

There are two types of power: personal and organizational. *Personal power* means that the individual has the knowledge, skills, mindset, and energy needed to meet the requirements of the situation. Professional Services personnel need a high degree of all these capabilities to meet the demanding needs of sophisticated customers. These capabilities will be outlined in Chapter Four and further discussed in Chapter Eight. Personal power is generated by the individual capacity to learn through training and on-the-job experience. Personal power is assumed—individuals do what's best in any given situation and think about the consequences (either positive or negative) later.

Organizational power means that the organization's leadership provides the individual with the resources, support, and information needed to make decisions during the moments of truth with customer personnel. Organizational leaders grant power by making sure that people have the right technology. These leaders allow their people to procure manpower or funding to get things done and continually encourage their people to use their own best judgment.

Customers of Professional Services expect the professionals they deal with directly to be able to make most decisions on their own and on the spot. Power must be focused at the point of customer contact. Focused power embodies both personal power and organizational power. The combination of the two creates highly skilled, motivated personnel with the resources, support, and information needed to make good business decisions fast.

The goal of focused power is for whoever is at the point of contact to make well-informed customer decisions immediately.

Flexible Structure

The demands of providing fluid information and focused power require that the supporting structure be flexible. The organizational structure must be simple, designate clear roles and responsibilities, and integrate all the rich information available to all people as fast as possible. The structure must support not only the Professional Services organization but also the *relationship* with the customer organization.

The ideal organization structure to implement the Professional Services strategy is the network.[6] The network operates with only minimal formal authority. Individual units or teams operate independently except for the essential task of documenting information useful to the entire organization. All nodes (teams) of the network have instant access to all the information (data bases, sales call activity, service logs, etc.) contained in the other nodes. The result is that everyone has immediate access to all the accumulated wisdom of the organization.

The network allows teams the speed and flexibility of a small independent group combined with the clout that comes with the resources and experience of a large organization. Teams have consistently proven their value in the fast-paced, changing field of Professional Services. Teams are used almost exclusively in top-performing Professional Service organizations such as system integrator EDS and the international consulting firm McKinsey.[7] Chapter Three will talk more about how teams work.

The goal of flexible structure is to allow maximum information flow and maximum power at the point of customer contact.

Fundamental Values

All strong organizations have a common set of shared values.[8] These values may be posted on walls and openly discussed, or they may surface only when certain problems or crisis occur. Fundamental values can be a powerful influencer of organizations. They provide a touchstone of how the organization views the world and what it considers important.

Fundamental values act as both boundaries and guides. Fundamental values explain where the borders of acceptable behavior are and what types of actions are appropriate "around here." They serve as a guide because they state in broad terms what is right and what is wrong.

---

6 Quinn, J B (1992). *Intelligent enterprise: A knowledge and service based paradigm for industry.* New York: Free Press.

7 Peters, T (1992). *Liberation management: Necessary disorganization for the nanosecond nineties.* New York: Alfred A. Knopf.

8 Kotter, J P, and J L Heskett (1992). *Corporate culture and performance.* New York: Free Press.

For example, an organization that has a fundamental value of honesty has a boundary that says behavior that does not demonstrate honesty is not acceptable. The fundamental value of honesty serves as a guide for all organization personnel. A person who does something dishonest will be fired immediately even if that person is a top-performing sales representative or a specialist in leading-edge technology. There is no other alternative. To do differently would violate the organization's code of ethics. The decision is guided by the fundamental value.

An organization that has a fundamental value of innovation proclaims that doing things differently and better is important. Successful members of this organization feel compelled to constantly challenge themselves to continually come up with better ideas. Business as usual violates this fundamental value. People who do not like innovation quickly ease themselves out of the organization because they soon realize that they do not have a good personal fit.

Fundamental values are extremely powerful influencers of behavior. It is the organization leader's responsibility to shape, define, articulate, and continuously enforce a set of fundamental values. Anytime a major issue arises, the fundamental values point the organization in the direction of the proper decision. Once fundamental values are integrated into the fabric of the organization, people immediately look to these values for the "right" behavior. There is more on fundamental values in Chapter Seven.

The goal of fundamental values is to create a common touchstone for organizational decision making.

The principles of fluid information, focused power, flexible structure, and fundamental values are an on-going guide to building the Professional Services business. The principles are brought to life when they are used to create effective processes.

ORGANIZING AROUND PROCESSES

Processes are the business definers of work. They determine which work activities are done and which are not. Processes are also the least understood and the least managed level of performance and therefore represent the biggest potential for improvement.[9]

FIGURE 2-2
Process

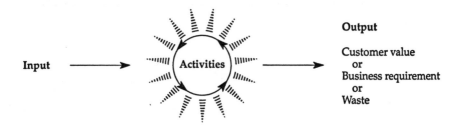

Input $\longrightarrow$ Activities $\longrightarrow$

Output

Customer value
or
Business requirement
or
Waste

In fact, organizations delivering Professional Services have a special challenge, since almost all Professional Services work is knowledge based. Research has determined that between 40 percent and 70 percent of all the efforts of knowledge workers add no value.[10] So about *one-half* of the typical Professional Services team's time, energy, and commitment is potentially wasted.

This waste occurs because people don't do the right work, do work the wrong way, or do work that should not be done in the first place. Although several things contribute to waste, the biggest culprit is the poor engineering and management of processes. Instead of the top-down, vertical world of functions, processes are the left-right, horizontal flow of work that cuts across functional barriers. Effective processes are vital to any high-performing Professional Services organization.

Figure 2-2 demonstrates that processes take inputs, sequentially perform activities, and create outputs. Process effectiveness depends on the quality of the output. Outputs do one of three things: create customer value, meet a business requirement, or add waste.

The customer defines value. If a process isn't positively impacting a customer, it isn't delivering customer value. The customer value test is simple—if the customer is willing to pay for it, it has customer value.

---

9 Rummler, *Improving performance.*

10 Harrington, H J (1991). *Business process improvement.* New York: McGraw-Hill.

Sometimes processes don't directly add value to a customer but are needed to run the supplier's business. For example, maintaining service records to meet ISO 9000 quality standards doesn't directly add value to the customer but meets a business requirement of assuring quality. The customer may require that your organization be ISO certified, but he or she probably won't pay extra for your certification. You have determined that it is a necessary cost of doing business. Therefore, maintaining service records is a business requirement.

In addition, any process mandated by law falls into the business requirement category. Filing OSHA reports, keeping expense copies for possible IRS audits, and documenting recruiting and hiring activities are all considered business requirements.

Processes that don't increase customer value or meet a business requirement create only waste. These processes not only contribute no value, but also consume resources that could be used for much better purposes. These processes get in the way of the important work of the organization and must constantly be challenged. Chapter Eight discusses the action steps to create effective processes.

Core processes are those processes most critical to generating customer value. A number of support processes, such as finance and information systems, support the core processes by contributing to business requirements. In Professional Services there are four core processes that maximize contribution to customer value; Chapter Three will define them.

Chapter Three

Defining the Processes

The Four Core Professional Services Processes
The Marketing Process
The Qualifying Process
The Selling Process
The Consulting Process
Special Challenges of Professional Services Processes

THE FOUR CORE PROFESSIONAL SERVICES PROCESSES

Since Professional Services organizations deal with highly complex companies facing complicated problems, a very sophisticated approach to managing the amount and intensity of information flow is required. Instead of the three functional silos typical of many customer contact organizations outlined in Chapter Two, Professional Services requires the redesign and reengineering of four core processes that maximize contribution to customer value.

Figure 3–1 displays the four core processes of Professional Services: marketing, qualifying, selling, and consulting. Each of the core processes is linked to the other to form a value-adding chain that starts with a connection to the overall business focus and concludes with a satisfied client that purchases again.

THE MARKETING PROCESS

There are major differences between the typical marketing function outlined in Chapter Two and the marketing process requirements

FIGURE 3–1
The Four Core Professional Services Processes

needed to implement Professional Services. An important reason for these differences is the potential customer base. A typical marketing organization may consider thousands or 10s of thousands of organizations as potential customers.

The number of accounts that have a business need for the sophisticated, knowledge-based solutions of Professional Services is limited. The bad news is that, depending on the business, the realistic potential may be a hundred accounts or less. The good news is that these potential customers have the ability to make very large, profitable investments in Professional Services solutions that improve their business.

Another significant difference is the investment in resources that the Professional Services strategy requires as compared to those of the traditional or value-added strategy. A large customer of a traditional organization might take less than one hundred hours *per year* to sell, service, and maintain adequate customer satisfaction. While an average-size customer of Professional Services may take more than one hundred hours *per week* to deliver on customer expectations.

Professional Services is extremely people intensive. Since the providers of Professional Services are seasoned, highly educated individuals, the sheer number of available qualified people limits the number of accounts a Professional Services organization can work with at any given time. These major differences mean that the role of marketing must be radically rethought.

FIGURE 3–2
Marketing Professional Services

Figure 3–2 displays the marketing process of Professional Services. The primary input to the Professional Services marketing process is known as *leads*—target accounts defined by the business focus that fit the general profile of the Professional Services customer. The output of the marketing process is called *suspects*—leads that have contacted the Professional Services organization and have shown interest in its capabilities.

Therefore, the purpose of the key activities of the marketing process is to turn leads into suspects. Key activities of the marketing process are researching, testing, and promoting.

The qualitative research emphasis of Professional Services marketing is dramatically different from typical quantitative market research. In-depth, rich information is generated *by account* to discover the specific business issues, attitudes, and expectations of numerous key people. The specific steps to amplifying the voice of the customer are detailed in Chapter Six. This in-depth understanding of specific accounts provides the information needed to determine the type of knowledge products and appropriate pricing strategies. There is more on products and pricing in Chapter Eight.

New knowledge products should be tested prior to promotion. The best place to test new ideas and concepts is with existing friends—accounts that usually love everything you do and are tolerant of the occasional mistake. This type of account enjoys experimentation and values joint projects that encourage innovation. Chapter Eight discusses the product development process for Professional Services.

Promoting the Professional Services organization is again quite different than promoting the typical organization. For the Professional Service marketing process to be effective, decision makers (harried executives from key organizations) must have enough interest to contact the Professional Services organization. Advertising, direct mail, and PR will not make this happen by itself.

In addition, no matter how well-researched and well-written the letter or how smooth and professional the phone call, **busy executives do not respond favorably to dialogues they do not initiate** —even if the business issue is a crystal-clear priority; even if the Professional Service organization is well known. Traditional prospecting tactics do not work in implementing a Professional Services strategy.

Therefore, the promoting activity is a vital one. Two things must happen before busy executives will contact an organization to discuss working together to solve major business problems. The decision makers must have some confidence in the organization and its capabilities and there must be enough urgency to get them to break away from business as usual to call.[1]

Word of mouth is the best way to promote Professional Services.[2] The three word-of-mouth activities of promoting are speaking, publishing, and networking.

Speaking at meetings, conferences, and symposia instantly provides a platform to display your organization's expertise. Thoughtful presentations showcase innovative customer success stories. The best presentations are the ones in which a customer speaks

---

[1] Hanan, M (1985). *Consultative selling.* 3rd ed. New York: AMACOM.

[2] Peters, T (1987). *Thriving on chaos: Handbook for a management revolution.* New York: Alfred A. Knopf.

instead of or in conjunction with a presenter from the Professional Services organization.

Publishing in journals and magazines provides the credibility of print. The emphasis again should be put on actual customer projects. Newsletters can also be used to highlight customer applications to Professional Services leads.

Networking uses the power of individual contacts to build personal credibility. Every well-established legal practice knows the value of community involvement of the firm's partners. Leading fund-raisers and serving on the boards of nonprofit organizations build personal relationships that can position the Professional Services organization as the one that is called when the timing is right.

Top management consulting firms have also networked extremely effectively by helping employees who are leaving their firm to find good positions with existing clients. These former employees maintain a strong bond to the consulting firm and help funnel more client business to the consulting firm.

Networking should also be a planned activity. Potential customers can be invited to a breakfast or lunch in which a good customer is present to discuss common issues. The customer can help you develop customer urgency and confidence in you by positively telling your story.

A conscious marketing effort should be made to network with the respected early innovators in your target industry that have successfully used your Professional Services solutions. Every opportunity should be sought to get them in front of potential customers.

There is a fourth very important promoting activity, but it occurs during the consulting process described later in this chapter. This promoting activity is exceeding customer expectations. Exceeding customer expectations is the most powerful way to grow the business and generate positive word of mouth. A conscious effort should be made to go above and beyond the expectations of certain (if not all) customers. It should be formalized in the form of an objective and should be built into the project plan. Exceeding customer expectations will produce a group of loyal, vocal champions that will go out of their way to help you succeed.

THE QUALIFYING PROCESS

Qualifying is the next core process of Professional Services. In the past, organizations included qualifying as a step in the overall selling process. When selling is straightforward and solutions are simple, qualifying is important but not vital.

Professional Services is an entirely different situation. The decision to marshal limited resources to pursue new business is vital to the success of the Professional Services organization. Qualifying determines how well you will grow and innovate; it deserves the same status and emphasis as the other three core processes.

Often in qualifying, a fast no is better than a slow yes. The worst thing that can happen is to sell an account that is not a good match. Satisfaction stays low; frustration increases; costs go up; and opportunities with other, better potential accounts, go by as additional resources are spent trying to satisfy an account that can't be satisfied by your solution and that should never have been sold in the first place.

FIGURE 3–3
Qualifying Professional Services

Figure 3–3 displays the qualifying process of Professional Services. Suspects, the output of the marketing process, are the inputs of the qualifying process. The output of qualifying is known as *prospects*—organizations that have a fair probability of being sold. Key activities of the qualifying process include researching, analyzing, and deciding.

Performing these three activities is greatly simplified when utilizing key success factors. Key success factors use the past experience of the Professional Services organization to describe the prime elements that help determine whether a suspect is worth pursuing.

Suspect research is geared toward uncovering information related to each factor. Research tactics start with gathering financial reports and promotional materials. Next is personal contact with people who have first-hand information and experience with the suspect. Likely contacts include people inside your organization, noncompetitive suppliers of the suspect, and suspect customers. Armed with this information, research activities evolve to talking with suspect personnel either on the phone or face-to-face.

Analyzing the research assigns a plus and minus score to each factor. Deciding determines the probability of a how easily the account can be sold and how good a match might develop. Management must then make the decision on the value versus the cost of pursuing the account further.

Figure 3–4 displays the completed key success factor assessment worksheet for Maximum Technologies, a fictitious account. Here is how it works. The first key success factor is importance to account. Your research convinces you that the issue of system redesign you are analyzing is a top business priority for Maximum. Management has committed to solve this problem. From your perspective, this is very positive, so you might score this factor a +4.

The next key success factor is business fit. From your past knowledge, you know that your Professional Services organization has proven experience working in Maximum's industry. However, you have never worked on all the aspects of this particular problem. You decide to score this factor a –1.

This approach is continued until all factors have been scored. Next, all the factors are added together to develop an overall key success factor success potential. The larger the positive number, the higher the probability of selling the suspect and of a good match. In the case of Maximum, your tally shows a success potential of +12, a good indicator of potential.

This overall success score helps you decide whether Maximum is a qualified prospect or not. It also visually displays factors that should be leveraged to take advantage of strengths and factors of weakness that must be minimized if the account is to be pursued for business. You decide that Maximum Technologies warrants becoming a prospect and you will try and sell it.

FIGURE 3–4
Key Success Factors

Key Success Factors Assessment Worksheet										
Date: 12–10–94					Account: Maximum Technologies					
Minimize −						Leverage +				
5	4	3	2	1	Importance to Account	1	2	3	(4)	5
5	4	3	2	(1)	Business Fit	1	2	3	4	5
5	4	3	2	1	Personal Fit	(1)	2	3	4	5
5	4	3	2	(1)	Credibility	1	2	3	4	5
5	4	3	2	1	Consulting Attitude	1	2	(3)	4	5
5	4	3	(2)	1	Competition	1	2	3	4	5
5	4	3	2	1	Access to DM	1	2	3	(4)	5
5	4	3	2	(1)	Funding	1	2	3	4	5
5	4	3	2	1	Importance	1	2	(3)	4	5
5	4	3	2	1	Timing	1	(2)	3	4	5

Success Potential = +12

Another advantage of using this assessment worksheet is that it provides a standard qualifying guideline for the organization and a common tool for coaching and account planning. A qualified prospect is now ready to be sold.

THE SELLING PROCESS

Effectiveness of all four core processes is important; effectiveness of the selling process is vital. Selling has never been an easy job; that is why top sales performers make the big bucks and go on incentive trips while the rest of the organization stays home. Salespeople have been portrayed as lone gunfighters, waging battles of constant rejection against tight-lipped customers and savage competitors. That explains why management has been more tolerant of the individualistic, quirky, and occasional prima donna behavior of some sellers.

Selling Professional Services is very different and much more demanding than traditional or value-added selling because of these five challenges:

1. *Complexity of customer issues.* The business issues that customers want to address through Professional Services are complex, messy, difficult to define, and often difficult to understand.

2. *Customization of the Professional Services product.* Every knowledge-solution is unique to each particular customer.

3. *Challenges of gaining commitment.* Multiple people across different functions and up and down several layers of management must be convinced of the value of the solution. Senior management must be sold on the financial return on investment.

4. *Coordination of the team.* Internal experts must be recruited and coached to help gain the sale.

5. *Cycle time of selling.* Selling cycle time must be planned, tracked, and managed to minimize the potentially huge selling costs of Professional Services.

Selling Professional Services greatly expands the skills normally thought of as being needed for traditional selling. Selling Professional Services requires a broad set of capabilities that are discussed in Chapter Four. However, new capabilities alone cannot meet these five challenges. A well-engineered and well-managed

FIGURE 3–5
Selling Professional Services

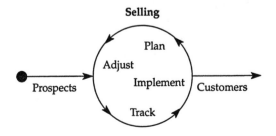

performance system must be in place to effectively implement Professional Services selling. Chapter Four addresses this important issue in more detail.

Figure 3–5 displays the selling process for Professional Services. It takes prospects and turns them into customers—organizations that have committed to a Professional Services solution. Key activities of selling include planning, implementing, tracking, and adjusting.[3]

Systematic planning is an imperative in Professional Services selling. The potential risks and rewards are too great not to plan carefully. The key account planner is a selling tool that helps increase the probability of selling success. It is also a tracking and coaching mechanism that shortens the selling cycle and maximizes resource utilization. The major input to the key account planner is the key success factor assessment sheet discussed earlier.

Tens of account team hours may go into the development of a solid key account plan. Figure 3–6 shows a completed (abbreviated) key account plan for Maximum Technologies.

Listed there are the elements of a good key account plan. Note that although there is a logical order to building the plan, the elements can be completed in any sequence. Since input on one element will probably impact another element, continual revision is expected. The concepts of key account planning are directly derived from the field of project management. Chapter Five discusses some of the special properties of projects and Chapters Seven and Eight provide more information.

Relationship Manager

One individual must have overall responsibility for successfully selling the account and managing the long-term relationship. That person is the relationship manager, who orchestrates the account team to meet selling objectives.

---

[3] The process steps for selling and consulting are modifications of the Shewhart cycle: plan, do, check, act. We refer the reader to William Eureka and Nancy Ryan's discussion of the use of policy and process deployment in effectively manage business activities: (1990. *The process driven business: Managerial perspectives on policy management*. Dearborn, MI: American Supplier Institute).

FIGURE 3–6
Key Account Planner

Date: 1–2–95   **Account:** Maximum Technologies

Relationship Manager:	• Alex Steele
Account Team:	• Zeke Kelly — systems expert • Kerry Storm — financial expert • Bill Starr — coach
Objective:	• Generate initial $100,000 commitment for system redesign by 4–2–95 at maximum selling cost of $25,000 (including time)
Opportunities:	• Issue very important to account • Looks like there will be access to the decision maker • Timing looks good
Risks:	• Business fit is a little stretch • Unsure of their attitudes toward consultants
Considerations:	• Maximum Technologies shuts down for two weeks each June • Kerry Storm is moving in February

Stakeholder Analysis:

Stakeholder	Role	Issues	Personality Type
	• Decision maker • Influencer • Implementer • Coach	• Business • Personal	• Dominant • Influencer • Steady • Compliance
Jan Owens, CIO	Influencer	• Technology, innovation • Look good to Tom	Influencer
Tom Smith, Pres.	Decision maker	• Cutting cost • Seen as running tight ship	Dominant
Nancy Ellis, Dir.–IS	Influencer	• Improve system performance • Keep job	Steady

Critical Events: • Visit customer
 • Needs assessment
 • Pilot project
 • Proposal

Account Team

Professional Services selling requires the abilities of more than one individual. The relationship manager recruits experts who have the special knowledge/skills needed to get the sale. These experts

FIGURE 3–6
Key Account Planner (concluded)

Date: 1–2–95		Account: Maximum Technologies	
Action Steps:			

What	Who	Time	When
Prepare for meeting with Jan	Alex	2 hours	1-7
Appointment with Jan	Alex	1 hour	1-14
Review Jan meeting	Alex	1 hour	1-16
	Bill	1 hour	
Plan customer visit	Kerry	3 hours	1-23
	Alex	1 hour	
	Bill	1 hour	
Customer visit	Alex	4 hours	1-31
	Kerry	4 hours	

may come from different areas inside the company such as service, marketing, engineering, finance, or wherever special skills/knowledge are needed. Experts may need to be outsourced if internal capabilities are not available or do not exist. An internal coach (usually a manager) should be on the team to provide guidance and remove organizational obstacles to getting things done.

Account Objectives

Specific, measurable, realistic, and motivating objectives should be in place around quality, time, and budget. Quality objectives should include both the volume and margin of the initial sale and account potential. Time objectives should target specific dates for getting the business. Budget objectives should lay out realistic cost of sale expenses, including a dollar amount for account team time.

Opportunities

Opportunities include the biggest plus factors uncovered completing the key success factor assessment form.

Risks

Risks include the biggest minus factors uncovered completing the key success factor assessment form.

Considerations

Considerations are any unique attributes specific to this selling situation.

Stakeholder Analysis

The stakeholder analysis critically reviews anyone outside the supplier organization that "has a stake" in the success or failure of your organization's making the sale. The analysis lists the stakeholders, their role, their primary business issues, their main personal issues, and their personality type. There could easily be a dozen or more stakeholders in a Professional Services sale. Key suppliers or even competitors might be included.

Critical Events

Critical events are the key actions that *the account takes* that lead directly to the sale. All accounts have a formal or an informal decision-making process when it comes to addressing major issues. Addressing critical events is first a matter of determining key actions that the account normally takes. Next, it is a matter of trying to eliminate, or alter, these key actions to determine the appropriate critical events. Critical events act as milestones toward accomplishing key account plan objectives.

Action Steps

Action steps list the steps that need to be taken to make sure that the critical events occur. Action steps should list the step, the individual from the account team who is responsible for it, the date the step is to be completed, and an estimate of the amount of time account team personnel will need to accomplish the step. All parts of action steps must be measurable.

Implementation is the systematic achievement of the action steps. Tracking is a regular, planned activity that starts the same time as implementation. The relationship manager monitors the progress of the team using the action steps developed in the plan. The team should meet regularly for the specific review of progress. Meetings can take place in person or through video, telephone, or electronic conferencing.

Progress review meetings are problem-solving meetings. One rule is certain: Things do not go as planned. These meetings provide the forum to analyze the existing situation and adjust accordingly. The questions that must always be asked in key account planning are: How can we leverage our strengths? How can we minimize our weaknesses? What can be done to compress the buying process?

An important consideration in the selling process is whether to pursue the business at all costs. The discussion of qualifying stated that a fast no was better than a slow yes. This maxim also has much value in selling. As account situations change, both new opportunities and new obstacles will arise. Professional Services

FIGURE 3–7
Consulting Professional Services

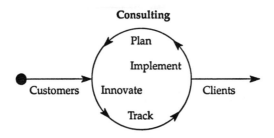

selling is a fluid process that must continually adjust to new situations. The relationship manager must continually ask the question whether to fish or cut bait. Limited selling resources demand that they be used in the highest potential accounts and not wasted chasing bad business.

Another vital task of the account team is estimating the cost of consulting projects. Any future possibility of profit depends on the accuracy of estimating. To estimate properly, the account team must be able to define both the personal and business issues of the account and help shape and define mutual and realistic expectations in solving them. These are high skill requirements based on experience and practice. Shaping and defining realistic expectations are vital elements to successful projects.

The final task is gaining a commitment to an agreement that has a high probability of meeting or exceeding the expectations of the account while providing your organization a fair return on investment. When this occurs, your organization has successfully turned a suspect into a customer, concluding the selling process.

THE CONSULTING PROCESS

Figure 3–7 displays the consulting process of Professional Services. The successful consulting process takes customers and turns them into clients. Clients are distinct from customers in that clients make a commitment to the Professional Services organization that goes beyond the initial sale.

Clients purchase more consulting solutions usually within a short period of time. Clients often provide an added benefit by recommending your Professional Services to prospects. See the discussion about promoting in the marketing process earlier in this chapter.

Turning customers into clients is absolutely critical in Professional Services. The large investment in selling must be leveraged to maximize performance. To gain client status, performance goals must be met or exceeded. For example, helping improve the sales productivity of customers 25% instead of the objective of 15% will certainly get their attention. Going out of your way to develop prospects for your customer is another way to exceed their expectations and turn a customer into a long-term client.

A project manager is chosen to lead the project team and has the dual responsibility of meeting the expectations of both the account and the Professional Services organization. In addition, the project manager coordinates with the relationship manager to make sure the project doesn't interfere with other projects or selling opportunities going on within the account. The project must not jeopardize other potential business.

Strong project management skills are needed to complete the key consulting activities of planning, implementing, tracking, and innovating. The execution of these activities parallels the steps discussed in the selling process. The project plan is built, implemented and tracked in a similar fashion.

Whereas in the selling process the fourth activity was adjusting, in the consulting process it is innovating. Innovation challenges the project team to deliver the knowledge product in such a way that it goes beyond expectations. Innovation uses knowledge to drive positive change in ways that exceed project objectives. This innovation can then be used profitably with other accounts and can uncover other opportunities for the client.

SPECIAL CHALLENGES OF PROFESSIONAL SERVICES PROCESSES

To be successful, all four of the core processes must be performed well. Some special challenges, however, are inherent in Professional Services processes. In manufacturing and other processes *inside* the organization, control can be maintained over inputs, goals, expectations, and specific activities. Professional Services processes occur both inside *and* outside the organization.

Selling and consulting are the most challenging processes to perform well because of the high degree of interpersonal contact required, the intensity of information involved, and the intricacy of defining and solving ambiguous problems. In addition, during the consulting process, the effective Professional Services team members are both delivering solutions for the existing project *and* uncovering the issues and needs necessary to sell the next consulting project.

The challenges inherent in Professional Services processes are as follows:

- The customer controls/influences/participates directly in many of the process activities.
- Customer expectations are shaped by Professional Services personnel.
- Customer expectations are subject to change, and they usually do.
- The customer's own buying/implementing processes are subject to change.
- The customer's buying/implementing processes vary among customers.
- Communication, coordination, and implementation are dynamic and complex.

Processes are the organizing mechanism of Professional Services. The four core processes all work together to maximize customer value. Effectively implementing Professional Services processes requires strong project management practices, talented people, and the performance systems to support them. Chapter Four discusses how to build the high-performance Professional Services team and the system needed to guide performance.

Chapter Four

Building the High-Performance Professional Services Team

The Good Old Days of Service
The Good Old Days of Selling
The Big Leap
The Four Critical Capabilities
Hire, Train, or Outsource
The Performance System

T he Professional Services strategy is selected, the principles of organizing are established, and the four core processes have been defined. Now it is time to build the high-performance team that will operate the processes. Performers must be developed and a performance system must be put in place to optimize performance.

Dramatic changes impacting sales and service personnel have occurred over the last 15 years. The original jobs that these performers were hired to do probably no longer exist. Let's start by looking at service.

THE GOOD OLD DAYS OF SERVICE

In the good old days of service, technical knowledge was king. The ability to accurately diagnose a hardware problem and efficiently perform the fix so that the customer was up and running quickly was the key ingredient. The services organization (and the customer) would overlook poor communication skills, sloppy appearance, and even rudeness if the technician solved the problem. In the early days of high unreliability, narrow product design, and crude diagnostic tools, the technically proficient service provider was often regarded as a hero. Many of today's service personnel started out in the field during these "good old days" of field services.

As product quality became dramatically better, the competition became tougher, and the customer became more sophisticated, the expectations of service personnel started to change. Off-site diagnostics evolved and the loosening of the manufacturer monopoly on service occurred. Technical expertise was still important but no longer important enough. The technical savvy needed decreased with the advent of simplified designs, well-written manuals, and expert systems. Service technicians were asked to manage their time better and be more efficient to improve service productivity. Organization as well as time and territory management were elevated in importance.

Managing the moments of truth became the next major focus because of the competitive need to improve customer satisfaction and develop new business. Customer satisfaction skills were seen as important for dealing with irate customers. Selling skills were recognized as important as the service organization discovered the need for selling services itself.

So the primary role of services personnel has changed from troubleshooting expert, to efficient technician, to salesperson with a quota. The jobs that most of the veterans on staff have now are radically different from the jobs they were originally hired to do. A few service personnel have adapted extremely well to the changes in role and responsibility. However, most are still in a state of transition, questioning their new responsibilities, unsure of their ability to perform them, and occasionally longing for the good old days.

THE GOOD OLD DAYS OF SELLING

In the good old days of selling, just being there was enough: make the sales calls, be friendly, dress well, do lunch. In the good old days, demand for product was high, price was not a major concern, and there was enough business for everyone. There actually were differences in the physical product and customers seemed to care about them.

The average salesperson knew the features and benefits of the product. The good salesperson knew the features and benefits of the competitor's products. To get ahead, the ambitious salesperson just worked more hours and made more calls. Customers wanted salespeople to know their product, be friendly, be honest, call ahead for appointments, and follow up on what they promise.

As times changed, so did the demands placed on the salesperson: tougher competition, more sophisticated customers, longer selling cycles, and pressures on price. Sales reps honed their selling skills and worked on becoming more "professional."

As the complexity of selling continued, sales cycles became longer still and even more unpredictable. More people were brought into the buying process and the final decision was being made higher and higher up in the customer organization. Competitors started selling service in an effort to differentiate themselves. Slower sales, leaner margins, and cutbacks in selling budgets put added pressure on sales organizations to make things happen. Sales reps were forced to address pricing and look for more ways to try to appear different against "me-too" competition. Talk to most veteran salespeople and they will tell you that a lot of the fun has been taken out of selling.

THE BIG LEAP

The role shift from the early days to the present is a big step for sales and service personnel. The role shift has created personal performance gaps that have to be addressed through changes in skills, knowledge, and attitude toward the business and toward the job.

The role shift required to implement Professional Services is a another major leap for existing sales and service personnel. The role of the Professional Services team is to systematically apply knowledge to improve performance that adds value both to the customer and to the team's own organization. This unique challenge dictates that Professional Services personnel possess all the capabilities

FIGURE 4–1
The Four Critical Capabilities

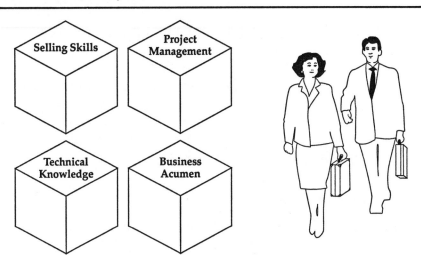

described earlier plus much more. **There is an extremely high probability that organizations starting up a Professional Services group do not currently have all the needed capabilities inside the organization.**

Figure 4–1 displays the four critical capabilities of selling skills, project management, technical knowledge, and business acumen that the Professional Services team must possess.

THE FOUR CRITICAL CAPABILITIES

Selling Skills

The selling ability of the Professional Services organization has the single largest impact on success. The Professional Services team must be able to diagnose, analyze, and succinctly discuss customer problems; develop the urgency to solve those problems; and commit customers to a realistic plan of action that will produce mutually beneficial results.

Professional Services selling is the highest order of selling. Usually the issues are difficult to put your arms around, the risks are not always known, and the solutions are intangible and difficult to envision. The commitment is highly influenced by reputation and the personal chemistry of the key account team with account personnel.

Selling Professional Services is not for everyone. Past experience with product sales is often more a detriment than a help. Professional Services selling demands a long-term, team approach. Many highly successful product salespeople either cannot or will not make the jump to Professional Services selling.

Project Management

No one individual has all the knowledge and skills needed to deliver complex Professional Services solutions, so Professional Services is organized around teams. In the core process of selling, the account relationship manager uses project management to build relationships, uncover problems, set objectives, map out activities, assign tasks, and monitor progress. In the core process of consulting when the solution has been sold, the project manager uses project management to meet quality, time, and budget objectives in the most efficient way.

Project management replaces traditional management by eliminating hierarchical barriers and focusing all efforts on the accomplishment of process objectives. Project management is ideal for dealing with the ill-defined, complex, ever-changing world of Professional Services issues.

Technical Knowledge

Technical knowledge is still a critical capability of the Professional Services team. In addition to the knowledge of products and the processes that surround them, technical knowledge in Professional Services may demand an in-depth understanding of inventory control, total quality management (TQM), market research, or financial analysis. This application-based knowledge is multi functional, and several different organization members may be called on to deliver on large projects.

Business Acumen

The solutions that Professional Services address affect customers' important business issues. Decisions about these business issues are made by customer executives. When it comes down to it, executives are concerned only about the performance of their business. Professional Services personnel must understand, think, and be able to talk the language of business. *The Wall Street Journal*, *Harvard Business Review*, and *Fortune* magazine are now their required reading.

HIRE, TRAIN, OR OUTSOURCE

A key output of implementing those steps is a performance profile that lists the specific knowledge and skills necessary for the Professional Services team. A very key decision must then be made: hire new people, train existing personnel, or outsource expertise. All three have special advantages and unique challenges. Chapter Eight discusses this decision in more detail.

Developing performers to master Professional Services processes is a continuous organizational commitment. Addressing existing performance gaps is vital to meeting today's expectations. Investing in the future development of personnel will prepare the organization for tomorrow's challenges and yield a long-term return to the business.

THE PERFORMANCE SYSTEM

Peter Drucker proclaims

the single greatest challenge facing managers in the developed countries of the world is to raise the productivity of knowledge and service workers. This challenge, which will dominate the management agenda for the next several decades, will ultimately determine the competitive performance of companies. Even more important, it will determine the very fabric of society and the quality of life in every industrialized nation.[1]

---

[1] Drucker, P F (1991). The new productivity challenge. *Harvard Business Review*. 69 (6), p. 69.

Most productivity improvement efforts focus on the individual. It is important that Professional Services team members have adequate knowledge and skill. However, only 15 percent of performance problems are individual performer problems and 85 percent are management problems. So no matter how competent the individual or the Professional Services team, it can contribute only 15 percent of the solution.[2] Professional Services performance must be viewed as a system with all the factors that influence the system taken into account.

Broadly defined, a *system* is the controls that are applied to a process to ensure that it is operating effectively and efficiently. As Rummler and Brache point out, "If you pit a good performer against a bad system, the system will win almost every time."[3]

It is management's responsibility to build the performance system to support the Professional Services team and improve productivity. Building the performance system includes creating clear performance specifications, determining a logical work flow, providing adequate resources, establishing consequences, providing feedback, and recognizing and rewarding excellent Professional Services performance. Figure 4–2 depicts the Professional Services performance system.

Create Clear Performance Specifications

All performance expectations of the Professional Services team must be clearly specified. Expectations—whether for managing an entire process such as selling, leading a client project, or performing a critical task—must be determined based on the factors of quality, time, and budget.

The Professional Services organization must focus on how effectively and efficiently it can meet performance expectations. The question becomes: What is the minimum amount of resources that can be expended to deliver the most time effective and least costly way to meet specifications? Efficiency and the elimination of waste are key components.

---

2 Deming, W E (1982). *Quality productivity, and competitive position.* Cambridge, MA: Cambridge Center for Advanced Engineering Study, Massachusetts Institute of Technology.

3 Rummler, G A and A P Brache (1991). *Improving performance: How to manage the white space on the organizational chart.* San Francisco: Jossey-Bass.

FIGURE 4–2
Professional Service Performance System

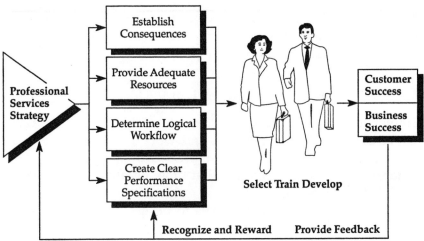

The Professional Services team should set its own performance specifications. Realistic specifications come from a good understanding of the existing customer and the combined past experiences of the Professional Services team. Strong documentation of previous experiences help set realistic benchmarks for performance standards. Measures must also take into account the hard business reality of the cost structure of the Professional Services organization combined with the revenue and profit expectations of senior management.[4]

Performance specifications must be quantifiable, understandable to team members, and attainable. Specifications must be balanced with the reality that the most easily attainable numbers are usually not the most appropriate.

Since core processes are the driver of the Professional Services organization, performance specifications must be set for each core process. The owner of the marketing process is responsible for producing a certain number of suspects during a certain period of

---

[4] Kuhlken, L E (1993). *Expanding professional services: A manager's guide to a diversified business*. Homewood, IL: Business One Irwin. Kuhlken provides an in-depth look at internal productivity measures.

time at such-and-such investment of time and money. That should be the key performance indicator. Marketing team members should be responsible for directly contributing to this objective. The same holds true for each of the other four core processes of qualifying, selling, and consulting. Clear performance specifications must be set out for each core process.

Determine Logical Work Flow

Similar to processes, jobs must be defined based on performing key activities. Often procedures and work practices are in place because of tradition. They don't necessarily support (and often hinder) doing the job right the first time. Because so much of the knowledge needed to do the job is resident in only the team members, they are the best individuals to design jobs and determine logical work flow.

It is management's responsibility to remove obstacles that get in the way of getting the work done the way the client wants it. The key questions are: Is the job design customer driven? How can the work be done simpler, easier, faster?

Provide Adequate Resources

It is the vital role of management to provide the necessary resources needed to meet performance expectations. The resources of Professional Services center on the principles of organizing discussed in Chapter Two. Personnel must have the power granted to them to make decisions fast that impact meeting customer expectations. They must have readily accessible information on customers, processes, and internal best practices. The communication process must allow for immediate interaction. The fundamental values must be in place to guide decision making. In addition, they must be supported by a team made up of other talented professionals.

Professional Services team members must also have realistic time to complete the job. Managers must continually adjust, shift, and level assignments to make sure that time frames are realistic. Team members must be given the tools needed to simplify work. Physical and electronic job aids "codify" the critical steps, best practices, or most common errors to ease and speed the achievement of goals. Useful tools for Professional Services application come from quality, project management, and other fields. Two examples of tools used in the Professional Services have already been mentioned: the key success factor assessment worksheet and the key account planner. A new tool is introduced later in this chapter.

Finally, Professional Services team members must be provided formal learning opportunities. Regular training and educational activities should be planned and scheduled.

Establish Consequences

Professional Services team members must know up front the consequences for either performing or not performing up to expectations. Positive consequences can take the form of incentive trips and bonuses or the prestige of being assigned to the most desirable or highest income-generating account.

Negative consequences should be in place for not meeting objectives, and positive consequences should be in place for meeting, or exceeding, expectations. Since successfully fulfilling the goals of Professional Services relies on a team, consequences should be team focused as well. Negative consequences could include less desirable project assignments, closer supervision of accounts, or even a decrease in decision-making authority. Once the consequences have been determined, they must be communicated in a way that all team members understand.

Provide Feedback

Management must provide objective feedback to team members. To be worthwhile, feedback must be relevant, accurate, timely, specific, and easy to understand. Managers should continually make available to all team members the status of quality, time, and budget goals. The most important feedback comes from clients as they communicate how well the Professional Services team is meeting their performance specifications. Formal client meetings should be scheduled to review the status of both existing projects and the overall client–Professional Services organization relationship.

Regular status meetings are an excellent way to update and motivate the team. It also provides a forum for the face-to-face sharing of information including uncovering potential problems and developing contingency plans in advance. Simple tracking charts prominently displayed are strong communicators and influencers of behavior. Charts should track client satisfaction, and productivity measures such as projected hours versus actual hours.

Finally, audits are a powerful feedback tool of the progressive Professional Services organization. Third-party audits, such as those required by ISO 9000 certification, determine whether processes and procedures are in place and if they are being followed. This type of audit determines accountability.

Another useful audit is performed by an expert who is not a member of the existing team. This individual or group can be a member of the Professional Services organization or a third-party expert. This audit looks at both the effectiveness and the efficiency of the processes being implemented. This approach brings in fresh ideas, challenges the status quo, and is an excellent way to develop inexperienced team members.

Recognize and Reward

Everyone likes recognition and the personal or physical rewards that accompany it. The vast majority of Professional Services personnel takes great pride in their capabilities. The most powerful recognition comes from on-going client and team member feedback. Ideally, all bonus compensation should be team focused. This creates an atmosphere of mutual support and subtle pressure not to let the team down. Incentive trips, premiums, and so on can be used effectively, but normally the greatest motivator of the professional is the personal pride of a job well done. Giving the professional an opportunity to write and publish articles, give presentations, and discuss the latest ideas in the field with outside peers at professional meetings are strong incentives.

Figure 4–3 displays the Professional Services performance checklist. This is a tool that helps give a rough analysis of how well the Professional Services performance system is operating. It should be used on an on-going basis and include input from all the members of the Professional Services team.

FIGURE 4–3
Professional Services Performance Checklist

	Never			Always	

Process, Project, or Task _____

THE SYSTEM

Create Clear Performance Specifications

		Never				Always
1.	Do team members clearly understand what is expected?	1	2	3	4	5
2.	Do team members feel expectations are attainable?	1	2	3	4	5

Determine Logical Workflow

3.	Is the workflow logical?	1	2	3	4	5
4.	Is interference to getting the job done minimized?	1	2	3	4	5

Provide Adequate Resources

5.	Do team members have the power to meet customer expectations quickly?	1	2	3	4	5
6.	Do team members have the information they need when they need it?	1	2	3	4	5
7.	Does the structure support performance?	1	2	3	4	5
8.	Do team members have enough time to complete required tasks?	1	2	3	4	5
9.	Do team members have the tools to do the job?	1	2	3	4	5

Establish Consequences

10.	Are clear consequences in place?	1	2	3	4	5
11.	Are consequences meaningful?	1	2	3	4	5
12.	Are consequences timely?	1	2	3	4	5

Provide Feedback

13.	Do team members receive relevant feedback?	1	2	3	4	5
14.	Is feedback accurate?	1	2	3	4	5
15.	Is feedback timely?	1	2	3	4	5
16.	Is feedback specific?	1	2	3	4	5
17.	Is feedback easy to understand?	1	2	3	4	5

Recognize and Reward

18.	Are team members adequately recognized for meeting or exceeding expectations?	1	2	3	4	5
19.	Are team members adequately rewarded for doing a job well done?	1	2	3	4	5

THE PEOPLE

Capabilities

20.	Do team members have the necessary knowledge and skills?	1	2	3	4	5

Capacity

21.	Are team members mentally, emotionally, and physically able to perform?	1	2	3	4	5

Total	(*Add up total score of 21 items*)	= _____
Average	(*Take total and divide by 21 to get average score*)	= _____
Grade	(A = 5, B = 4, C = 3, D = 2, F = 1)	= _____

Performers are the implementer of the Professional Services processes. Whether training existing employees, hiring new personnel, or outsourcing expertise, the Professional Services team must be competent in the four critical capabilities of selling, project management, technical knowledge, and business acumen. A strong performance system is necessary to support the team and optimize results.

II

ACCELERATING IMPLEMENTATION

C reating the Professional Services organization is a challenging task fraught with complexity, ambiguity, and numerous
problems. Part II outlines how to address implementation in a
clear, straightforward way. It explains how to minimize risks and
leverage opportunities. It provides the guide on how to implement
Professional Services quickly and effectively. Step-by-step actions
are outlined with supporting tools provided and explained.

Chapter Five

Managing the Transition

There's No Place like Home

Horror Stories

The Transition Force Field Analysis

The Professional Services Transition Project

The Transition Project Team

Managing the Transition

C reating the high-performance Professional Services organization means moving from the existing "business as usual" model in place today to the "business of tomorrow" model of Professional Services. As discussed in previous chapters, this means a new strategy, different organizing principles, distinct core processes, focused team approach, and an accountable management system.

Once the decision is made to offer Professional Services, our natural tendency is to jump right in with both feet and follow the Nike approach to "just do it." Announce to the world that you are now a Professional Services organization. Distribute brochures and run some ads. Then wait for the customers to come.

Sadly, just flipping the switch won't transform the business overnight. To get to the business of tomorrow means that a major transition must occur. An example may help uncover the challenge of transition.

THERE'S NO PLACE LIKE HOME

Imagine that you and your family live in a quaint, old, traditional home. You have lived in it for many years, and it has served your needs well. Yet in the last few years, you have become dissatisfied.

Your dream is to live in a high-tech contemporary home. A built-in surround sound system, Jacuzzi, and recreation room are on your wish list. For practical reasons you decide to keep the existing house and continue to live there while the extensive remodeling takes place.

Although you have never tackled a project like this before, you decide to do it yourself. You are pretty handy and a quick learner. Besides, why pay expensive professionals? Your kids can help. You buy some books, talk to friends, charge up your Makita power drill, and head for the local lumberyard.

The day the first wall is removed, your doubts begin. You start to feel that this is a little larger undertaking than you originally thought. After several weeks you start to feel stressed and dread coming home at night from your real job. Progress is dreadfully slow. Mistakes are made and work has to be redone.

Family tempers rise and comments start flying: The house will never be done. The cost is much more than we thought. The old place wasn't all that bad. I never wanted to do it in the first place!

The temptations that go through your head include quitting while you are ahead (translation: stop before things get worse), moving in with your in-laws, hiring a general contractor to manage the project, and running off to Key Largo. All these options sound better than dealing with the present situation.

The problem is that you have been living in between: in between the comfortable old home of the past and the preferred, new home of the future. During this time, neither exists. In the absence of any stability, you and your family feel a variety of emotions including anger, despair, and helplessness.

Anyone who has ever lived between homes, jobs, or personal relationships can quickly identify with this time of transition. It just doesn't feel good.

HORROR STORIES

There is a basic similarity between the remodeling example and a business making the transition to Professional Services. Both involve change and the resistance that naturally occurs whenever change is present. Resistance comes about because of confusion, lack of clarity, and not having the special skills needed for this in between state. Left unmanaged, this resistance always leads to either the disruption, disabling, or death of the transition effort.

The following are a few real-world examples of what can happen when the transition is not dealt with properly. All of these examples resulted in the delay, demoralization, or demise of Professional Services:

- The telecommunications company that invested heavily to create a sales distribution network to sell Professional Services without having the delivery capabilities that customers wanted.
- The office products company that hired outside consultants to deliver Professional Services before the sales organization acquired the skills to sell it. Now the consultants sit around making big bucks.
- The software company that started advertising and marketing consulting services in hopes of developing a Professional Services capability sometime later.
- The supplier to the automotive industry that developed Professional Services but couldn't get its customers to pay for them.
- The computer manufacturer that dropped Professional Services after three years, organized sales around telemarketing a "hot box," and dropped field service altogether.
- The service manager who thought that given enough time, he could implement Professional Services himself. He waited too long and was fired.

These organizations wasted valuable, limited resources because they didn't think through the impact of transition.

THE TRANSITION FORCE FIELD ANALYSIS

In attempting to implement any plan, one must be aware that there are forces working for and against the accomplishment of the plan. The homeowner quickly found several forces getting in the way of successfully completing his remodeling. He also felt the positive effect of forces such as the desire for enjoying his new Jacuzzi after a stressful day at work.

Force field analysis is a technique that facilitates the identification of all the major forces that affect the accomplishment of a specific action or plan. Force field analysis helps examine and then select action steps most likely for success.

The steps to force field analysis entail the following:

- Thinking through a plan and a possible course of action.
- Identifying the forces that have the biggest potential impact on success or failure.
- Scoring the forces as either negative or positive.
- Leveraging the strongest positive forces and minimizing the strongest negative forces.

For example, the key success factor assessment worksheet described in Chapter Three is a force field analysis. The force field analysis technique is a very powerful tool. It should be used anytime an important project or plan is being considered. If the homeowner in the remodeling example had performed a force field analysis before his first trip to the lumberyard, he might have executed the remodeling quite differently. He would have foreseen obstacles and figured out ways to avoid them or decided not to do the remodeling at all.

Our consulting experience shows that there are certain forces that have a major effect on the success or failure of the transition to Professional Services. Figure 5–1 displays the Professional Services transition force field analysis.

Senior Management Commitment

Senior management see the trends and want to take action. They are eager to move ahead into just about anything that promises to address the issues of lowered sales revenue and shrinking profit margins.

Often senior management are the drivers of Professional Services. They hear about Professional Services success stories through a journal article or a seminar or from other business executives and decide that Professional Services is the way to go. They put someone in charge and then move on to the next decision. The initial commitment to the concept is made, but often an under-

FIGURE 5–1
Professional Services Transition Force Field Analysis

Minimize −						Leverage +				
5	4	3	2	1	Senior Mgt. Commitment	1	2	3	4	5
5	4	3	2	1	Team Buy-In	1	2	3	4	5
5	4	3	2	1	Customer Value	1	2	3	4	5
5	4	3	2	1	Leadership	1	2	3	4	5
5	4	3	2	1	Adequate Resources	1	2	3	4	5
5	4	3	2	1		1	2	3	4	5
5	4	3	2	1		1	2	3	4	5
5	4	3	2	1		1	2	3	4	5
5	4	3	2	1		1	2	3	4	5
5	4	3	2	1		1	2	3	4	5

Success Potential = _____

standing of Professional Services and the challenges of implementation are lacking.

With Professional Services, senior management must bankroll and stand behind a totally new business that usually runs counter to how they learned the business. Without the necessary education, they probably perceive Professional Services tactically, as an extension of the current business rather than strategically, as a competitive differentiator that affects several areas of operation.

Speed is an issue. Unless concrete results occur fairly quickly (money in the bank), senior management have a tendency to lessen support. They can either pull the plug altogether to terminate Professional Services or cut back funding to terminally wound the organization. Keeping senior management's attention and interest is vital to successful transition to Professional Services.

Team Buy In

Most sales and service personnel have been around the business world awhile. Some greet the announcement of a move to Professional Services very positively. Often top sales and service performers are already providing some elements of Professional Services without getting paid for it. Members of this elite group have seen the power of delivering Professional Services to customers and get personal satisfaction from the process. They get excited that the rest of the business is finally catching up to them.

Most often, however, the announcement of a new Professional Services organization is met with great skepticism. Cynically, employees talk about the come and go of programs of the month, such as World Class Performer, The Customer is Number One, and Building the Total Quality Future.

The reason for this cynicism is that team members are scared. They know that something will happen and they have read about massive right sizing in other companies in their industry. They are justly concerned about keeping their job.

Team members quickly realize that if the business does move ahead with implementing Professional Services, this could mean major changes for them. They will have to commit to a radical shift in roles and responsibilities, try to do things they weren't hired to do, and change their relationships with customers and with one another.

When Professional Services is announced to them either in a group or one on one, they play their cards close to the vest. They hide their doubts about why Professional Services may not work. They don't share their personal concerns about their own capabilities to do the new job—whatever that job is.

They nod their heads, say that Professional Services make perfect sense, and swear allegiance to the new team. Yet one of the main reasons that Professional Services doesn't get off the ground is that the team members never bought into the concept in the first place. They drag their feet and cling to doing things the way they did them in the good old days. Often the feeling is that if they can just wait it out, senior management will move on to follow a new fad. Yet without their buy in and support, Professional Services will fail.

Customer Value

As discussed in Chapter Three, the customer defines value. Sometimes customers see the potential value of Professional Services so clearly that they demand that someone provide it. They visit suppliers, offer resources and incentives, and twist arms in an effort to get their major business problems solved.

Sometimes Professional Services products are developed and launched but the customer doesn't want to buy them. Assumptions about what customers want and will pay for are wrong. There are numerous potential reasons. One is that the Professional Services offerings are really only an extension of existing services. They are just an attempt to package old solutions in a new bag. Customers are being asked to pay for services that have been delivered free in the past. These solutions fail the test of being knowledge products that positively impact the customer's business.

Sometimes customers don't believe the Professional Services products will meet their needs. Customers may have indicated that they will pay for Professional Services, but when it comes right down to it, they won't. Sometimes customers want the Professional Services but believe that the price is too high. Many customers resist altering their roles in working with the company. They resist changing from passive, uninformed observers to active, knowledgeable participants. Let's face it, you can have the best Professional Services in the world, but if the customer doesn't buy it, you haven't accomplished anything.

All of these problems can be avoided if the steps outlined in Chapter Six are followed.

Leadership

The individual tasked with leading the Professional Services transition has a marvelous opportunity to provide a major contribution to the business by creating the organization of tomorrow. Personally, the transition to Professional Services provides a wonderful chance to learn through this once-in-a-lifetime experience and to gain a lot of visibility in doing it.

However, just like team members, leading the transition to Professional Services is a major change in roles and responsibilities.

Often it is hard for the person responsible to know where to start. Just understanding what Professional Services is has been unclear. Until this book, there has been no definition of Professional Services applicable to sales and services, nor has there been a step-by-step approach to implementation.

Leading the transition requires new capabilities. The ideal credentials are very impressive: Professional Services guru, master persuader, effective project manager, experienced trainer, capable coach, and competent practitioner of transition management. Not many individuals fill this description. More on this later in the chapter.

Another problem is that many times the ownership of Professional Services is murky. Should sales, service, or marketing be responsible? Clear objectives and accountability haven't been established. One person needs to be accountable for the transition to Professional Services and be given or allowed to acquire the power necessary to do the job.

In addition to all of this, this transition leader often is saddled with running today's business while trying to build tomorrow's. The leader is so caught up in the old business that he or she never gets around to doing the hard work needed to create the Professional Services organization. The competition comes in, establishes, and then dominates the market for Professional Services.

Strong leadership is vital to the successful transition to Professional Services. To successfully launch Professional Services, the leader must concentrate on understanding the transition forces, gaining adequate resources, and recruiting the right team.

Adequate Resources

In most organizations there are *potentially* more than adequate resources available to support important strategic initiatives. However, it is simply amazing that billion-dollar companies will spend millions of dollars on capital equipment for manufacturing but balk at investing a fraction of that amount to launch a new business vital to company success. Sadly, all too often, no new money is budgeted at all. It is assumed that Professional Services can fund its own implementation from consulting revenue alone. "Bootstrapping" is idealized as the macho way to fund a project.

Management forgets, ignores, or never considers that it will probably take 6 to 18 months to start generating substantial revenue.

All of these forces need to be addressed. Using the force field analysis as a tool, the forces should be thought through and scored. As Figure 5–1 shows, blank spaces are on the force field analysis form to allow for special situations. This provides a fairly objective look at the overall probability of success or failure of transitioning to Professional Services. Plans must then be made to minimize negative forces and leverage positive ones.

The best way to deal with these forces is to create a special Professional Services transition project supported by adequate time and resources.

THE PROFESSIONAL SERVICES TRANSITION PROJECT

FIGURE 5–2
Professional Services Transition Project

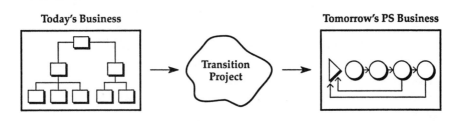

Figure 5–2 shows the transition from the existing business of today to the Professional Services business of tomorrow. In this model, both today's business and tomorrow's business are stable. In today's business, customers, senior management, and the people of the organization all know what to expect, and everyone is experienced with how things are done. In tomorrow's business, customers, senior management, and the team are all adjusted and comfortable with Professional Services.

The challenge is that a period of transition must occur "in between." Just like the remodeling homeowner discovered, the transition can be messy, discomforting, stressful, and very unproductive.

The solution to this challenge is to treat the transition as a special project. Thinking about the transition as a project requires us to examine some important considerations. First, a project has a set beginning and a set end; this time of confusion must not go on forever. Second, a project is made up of a number of interrelated tasks that cannot be done by any one individual, so a team must be created. Third, a project, by definition, is unmanageable. *Project management* is really a misnomer. With all the unforeseen changes that occur in implementing any complex project, the most you can hope to do is *guide* the project to the desired conclusion through smart planning by smart people. Contingencies must be thought through and be ready to implement. Fourth, although the project may be unmanageable, it is up to the project manager to accomplish project objectives.

The vehicle of project management is the project plan. The project plan starts with objectives based on quality, time, and budget. Next, a definition of the project that frames its scope is developed. The project team is identified and general roles and responsibilities outlined. Next, strengths and risks concerning the successful completion of the project are listed. Stakeholders are identified along with their issues and personalities. Critical tasks and project milestones are established with the people responsible for each task determined and completion dates listed. Finally, contingency plans are put together to address the important and probable obstacles that will surface during the project.

Creating the transition plan starts immediately on selecting Professional Services as a strategy. The plan is finalized at the end of the blueprinting phase discussed in Chapter Seven.

THE TRANSITION PROJECT TEAM

After reviewing the Professional Services transition force field analysis, the transition leader thoughtfully chooses the transition project team. Most of the money needed to fund the Professional Services transition is for people. The "know-how between the ears" or "juice" is what matters. Special efforts must be made to recruit people with the right know-how. The force field analysis helps determine the size, time commitments, and juice needed to get the job done.

Most organizations must look to outside resources to help staff the transition project for two reasons. The first is that it is rare to have all the Professional Services transition management capabilities resident in the organization. Transition management requires expertise in Professional Services, selling skills, project management, research techniques, training, coaching, negotiating, and facilitation.

The second reason is that the transition project requires hundreds of hours of intensive work spanning 6 to 18 months. Adding that workload to already busy people slows and reduces the effectiveness of the transition and also negatively impacts the performance of their regular jobs. Internal project people must dedicate a percentage of their time to the transition project. It is important to spell out in writing that Joe will spend 50 percent of his time, Mary 30 percent of her time, and so on. A few hours here and a few hours there won't do it. Senior management and the rest of the organization quickly lose patience when results are slow in coming.

The right project team can leverage the positive transition forces and help minimize the negative forces. Treating the transition as a special project is the correct approach to move the organization to Professional Services. With the team in place, it is time to manage the transition.

MANAGING THE TRANSITION

Figure 5–3 displays the four proven phases of successful Professional Services transition projects. The four phases of discovery, blueprinting, achievement, and tracking work together to manage the transition and accelerate Professional Services implementation.

Discovery is the research phase of the transition to Professional Services. It provides the information needed to motivate people and the organization to change. The two elements of discovery include amplifying the voice of the customer and assessing business issues.

Discovery is critical to the understanding of customer value. It is vital to Professional Services product development and pricing

FIGURE 5–3
Managing the Transition: The Four Phases

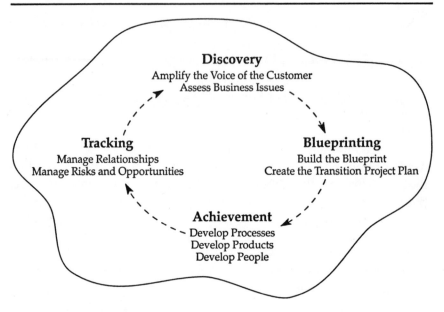

strategies. It also provides needed information to gain and accelerate senior management commitment and the buy-in of the team. A
successful discovery stage makes the life of the Professional Services leader much easier. Chapter Six discusses the discovery
phase in more detail.

Blueprinting helps create a new Professional Services strategy
and mindset. Participants struggle with the information gathered
during discovery to develop a new and motivational direction
based on areas of excellence and opportunity. The blueprinting
phase ignites senior management commitment and the buy in of
the Professional Services team. It also adds detail to the transition
project plan and directs the achievement phase to the highest priorities. Blueprinting sharpens the focus of your Professional Services efforts to optimize your resources and improve the odds of
success. Chapter Seven discusses the blueprinting phase.

Achievement applies critical resources to make the new Professional Services strategy a reality. The products are defined and

priced, processes are determined, performers are developed, stakeholders are managed, and problems and opportunities are handled. Implementing the achievement phase is discussed in Chapter Eight.

Tracking measures Professional Services transition project performance against established objectives and expectations. It provides continuous feedback that allows the Professional Services transition team to learn, improve, and make necessary modifications. Tracking is discussed in Chapter Nine.

Leading the transition to Professional Services is a complex, challenging mission for the individual tasked with this responsibility. Many obstacles exist. Strong motivation is needed to change the business-as-usual habits people develop over many years. Outside expertise is usually required to effectively manage the transition project and implement key activities.

Creating a high performance Professional Services organization entails changing yesterday's business into tomorrow's. All elements of the Professional Services system must be considered and planned for, even though most elements will create some resistance and confusion as they are implemented. The key is to plan for and manage the "in-between" time to successfully execute the Professional Services transition project.

Chapter Six

Phase 1: Discovery

The Problem with Traditional Market Research
Amplify the Voice of the Customer
Voice of the Customer Example
Assessing Business Issues
Business Issues Example

I n Chapter Five we said that gaining the buy in of senior management, the customer, and sales and service personnel is critical to managing the transition to Professional Services. Knowledge is power, and the Professional Services transition project team needs knowledge to gain the commitment of these key players. **At the outset of the transition project, it is extremely doubtful that the necessary information is already available inside the organization.**

Discovery is the research phase of the transition project; it serves two purposes. The first is to confirm that the Professional Services strategy is the best choice among the three strategies discussed in Chapter One. The second purpose is to uncover the minimum amount of rich information necessary to create a strong, realistic transition plan. Professional Services information is gathered by amplifying the voice of the customer and assessing business issues.

To gain this information, the right research approach is necessary. In our experience, the traditional market research approach is not appropriate.

THE PROBLEM WITH TRADITIONAL MARKET RESEARCH

Traditional market research techniques are widely used and have been successfully applied for years, especially in product-oriented consumer industries. These methods work well for sizing markets, segmenting industries, and identifying general trends and patterns.

Traditional market research methodologies are based on deductive methods and are basically abstract, both in theory and in the "numbers-driven" conclusions they reach. These quantitative methods focus on narrow definitions and limited variables. By statistical design, they eliminate the impact of context or culture on any subsequent findings.

Because of these constraints, faceless subjects rather than flesh and blood people are the ones analyzed. To retain any sense of "objectivity," the researcher must stand miles away from the data and the subjects who provide the data.

The market researcher's credo is "you can't argue with the numbers!" The problem is you can't motivate yourself—or anyone else, for that matter—to action with statistically generated "facts."

Traditional market research is adequate for learning about broad-based market and consumer issues, but it is woefully *inadequate* when it comes to learning about the specific issues and the needs of complex, key accounts for which Professional Services is a solution. In addition, a leather binder full of statistics doesn't have much power to excite and commit executives, let alone spur team members or accounts into action. Traditional market research is inadequate to drive the engine of transition.

Figure 6–1 compares traditional market research to discovery research. The traditional quantitative approach views research from a distance in a cool, cognitive fashion. The qualitative emphasis of discovery, on the other hand, relies on information provided in context by the people who use, sell, and buy your products. It is up close and personal. Because it's an approach that amplifies the voices of the people researched (rather than merely quantifying it), discovery deals directly with words and actions and gets at the underlying issues, feelings, and meanings.

Discovery focuses on the vital few rather than the useful many. Instead of the broad and thin approach of surveys and indexes,

FIGURE 6–1
Traditional Market Research versus Discovery Research

Traditional	Discovery
Quantitative	Qualitative
Distant	Up Close and Personal
Facts	Feelings
Useful Many	Vital Few
Broad and Thin	Thick and Deep
Ho-Hum	Call for Action

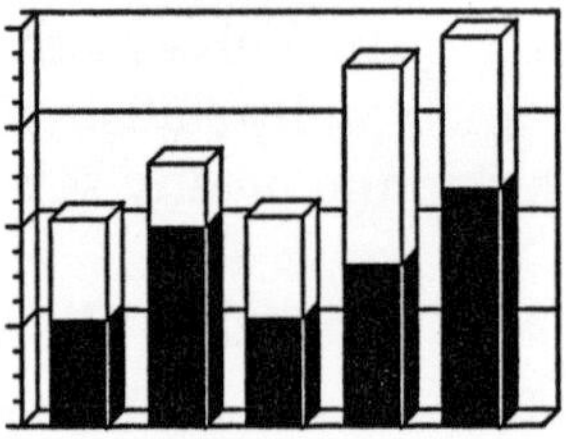

discovery provides the thick and deep analysis of concentrating efforts on a few selected accounts. The abstract printouts of traditional market research reports often leave a ho-hum response and limited desire for change. The colorful, pointed findings of discovery research delivered in the actual words of participants elicit a warm, visceral response with a motivating call for action.

With discovery research you don't have to worry about random samples, tests of variance, or regression analysis. Your goal is not to prove general theorems but to understand in-depth the specific insights of the people that are the most critical to your future. Since Professional Services focuses on those key, complex organizations, discovery research is an ideal fit.

AMPLIFY THE VOICE OF THE CUSTOMER

Amplifying the voice of the customer (VOC) utilizes the discovery research methods of in-depth personal interviews and focus groups. These qualitative research techniques provide rich, thick information that has the power to stimulate change and motivate people to action. Amplifying the VOC provides an understanding of the following information about key accounts:

FIGURE 6–2
Amplify the Voice of the Customer

1. Select key accounts
2. Interview
3. Transcribe
4. Analyze
5. Communicate

- Issues.
- Expectations of suppliers.
- Measurement of performance.
- Likes/dislikes of your organization.
- Recommendations for improvement and innovation.
- Comparison with top competitors.
- Attitude toward Professional Services.
- Decision-making process.

This information helps prioritize efforts and build the momentum for change. Properly orchestrated, it can be completed in just a few weeks. Figure 6–2 lists the steps to amplify the VOC using face-to-face interviews (focus groups can augment or replace face-to-face interviews, depending on the situation).

The five steps include select key accounts, interview, transcribe, analyze, and communiucate.

1. *Select key accounts.* The Professional Services transition project team selects accounts that are either existing customers or high-potential prospects. The most important consideration is that the accounts look like a good business fit for the future. Criteria might include potential dollar volume, geographic dispersion, industry position, type of culture, existing relationships, and so on. To maximize later buy-in, choose high-visibility accounts with name recognition that will capture senior management's attention. Wisely chosen, three to six accounts are adequate to research.

It is important to talk to a number of people at different levels and in different functions inside the account. Depending on the

situation, individuals to interview might include people from pur-
chasing, quality, engineering, information systems, product development, middle management, senior executives, and the actual
people who work with or are affected by the knowledge products
of Professional Services. Normally, between 6 and 12 individuals
per account should be selected.

2. *Interview.* The individual interviews start by positioning the
purpose of the interview, describing how the information will be
used, and explaining the value to the interviewee. Audio taping is
much preferred over note taking because it captures the exact
words of the interviewee and allows the interviewer to listen and
concentrate on the discussion. Most interviewees do not have a
problem with being audio taped if the interview has been properly
positioned.

Next comes in-depth questioning. Issues, expectations, likes,
dislikes, and competitive information are all uncovered. Interviewees are asked for stories to illustrate points. Questions to determine issues might include the following: What are your three top
problems? Why are they important? Give me an example. What is
the cost of not fixing them? What is your current plan for attacking
these challenges? In which areas are you looking for outside expertise? What are your expectations of an outside expert? Who have
you worked with in the past? What did you like about that experience? What didn't you like? Interviewees are encouraged to
expand on their comments and give examples and details.

Interviewees are asked to explain roles and responsibilities, outline decision-making processes, and make recommendations to the
Professional Services organization. Depending on the situation
(see the discussion of product and pricing in Chapter Eight), interviewees may be asked to weight the value of key service elements,
compare vendors in terms of capabilities, and assess value-to-price
relationships.

Typical interviews last about 45 minutes.

Toward the end of the session, interviewees are told what the
next actions will be. Closing this information loop is critical. Interviewees have spent their valuable time, and they want to how
their input will be used. An account review process is a powerful
way to do this. Implementing an account review process will be
discussed later in the chapter.

In some situations, as a final step, the interviewer asks to capture a few of the interviewees' most powerful comments on video. Using a hand-held video camera, 2 to 5 minutes are taped right then and there. Later how these snippets of customer video can be a powerful motivator for change will be discussed.

3. *Transcribe.* The audiotape is taken back and transcribed word for word. Transcripts typically range in length from 5 to 15 pages. Often the transcription is sent back to the interviewee to verify the information and to have the opportunity to give more input. Not only does this usually improve the quality of the information but also it gets the interviewee more involved and committed to the process.

4. *Analyze.* When all the interviews are completed, a thematic analysis of the transcripts is completed. Phrases that represent key concepts and issues are sorted and categorized. We recommend that all members of the transition team participate in this analysis.

The findings of the study are developed using the very words of customer personnel. The audio or video (if it has been shot) is edited to help tell the customer's story in a vivid, powerful way.

5. *Communicate.* The information gained will be a powerful input to the blueprinting process discussed in Chapter Seven. At that time, a broad group of company personnel will be exposed to the VOC and grapple with the information. However, sometimes the information won't wait that long. Often, unexpected, important information that demands immediate action is uncovered. For example, while doing Professional Services discovery research for a client, we uncovered the fact that its customer was in the process of dropping our client's hardware and going to a competitor. Quick action was able to halt the loss of a $2 million hardware account.

In addition, accounts expect a quick follow up once the interviews are complete. A potent approach is through an account review. The analyzed VOC information is presented and discussed to the account team composed of sales, service, marketing, and possibly other areas of the business. The account team grapples with the issues, explores options, and develops a plan of action and an account presentation.

This presentation is given to key personnel inside the account. It shares the findings and indicates planned next steps. It is a marvelous tool to open communication and strengthen the bonds with the key account. The process gives all participants a much greater understanding of the account and the current relationship. As you may have guessed, it is also a wonderful qualifying and selling device.

VOICE OF THE CUSTOMER EXAMPLE

A client of ours trying to negotiate the information highway saw a potentially lucrative Professional Services opportunity within a marketing group of its existing hardware/software customers. To test out the viability of Professional Services in this situation, four accounts (all customers in this case) were identified as targets for the voice of the customer research. The four accounts were geographically dispersed, had very large potential usage for Professional Services, and were recognized by top management as important customers.

The transition project team selected a cross-section of account personnel with whom to talk. Letters explaining the purpose of the research were sent to the people selected to be interviewed. These letters were followed up with personal phone calls to answer questions and confirm appointments. The issue of anonymity and use of the data were discussed thoroughly. The individuals were told that although information from the conversations would be utilized by the client team, the information would remain anonymous. How the insights would be used to improve the ability to satisfy the account's needs was discussed in broad detail. All but one of the selected people were open to sharing their perceptions.

We interviewed eighteen individuals representing multiple roles and responsibilities from within the four accounts. Sixteen of the interviews were face to face and 2 were lengthy telephone interviews. Thirteen of the interviews were audio taped, although three individuals were uncomfortable with this approach. In these instances notes were taken.

At the end of the interview, the researcher asked if the individual could summarize a few specific points on videotape. In this instance, only two people (an unusually low number) were willing to participate in videotaping.

The audio tapes were transcribed generating 150 pages of customer input. Next the researcher deleted names and references from the transcripts to hide the identity of interviewees.

"Anonymous" transcriptions were divided equally among the five members of the transition project team. Each team member was instructed to read the transcripts very carefully and to manually highlight or electronically select phrases that contained powerful information. Next, they were asked to group these phrases by themes, maintaining the actual language of the interviewee. They were told to be prepared to present their analysis to the team. Each project team member took about 10 hours to read and analyze the VOC material. There was a little complaining about the amount of work that went into this task.

The transition team met for one day to review the information. One by one, the team members posted on the wall the actual cutout customer phrases from the transcripts clustered into categories. They gave their reaction to the interviews and explained their feelings. We followed this up with our own analysis of the data. The two perspectives confirmed the seriousness of a number of problems, the significance of the Professional Services solution, and the urgency to take action.

Here are a very few representative excerpts from transcripts. There were a few surprises.

> You know, I'm here all day and they have not contacted me now. You know when you are designing a kitchen, you ask cooks what they need. I would like to see more of that. If you are going to design a system, you want to design something that the users are going to use.
>
> I really want to have ownership. The system is part of my business, a very important part of my business, and I feel outside of it.
>
> I'm feeling that I have to baby-sit my system. I feel I can't trust it to give me what I need.
>
> When we first tried to get this thing going, we had no help at all. It was basically one hand didn't know what the other hand was doing, and it seemed as if they didn't care what we were doing.
>
> Company A always seems to have a better pool of people to draw from than the other vendors. I've been saying that all along. They are creative, a little crazy, you know? You need that.
>
> I think it's a good product. The weaknesses are the training and support, the communication, and coordination.
>
> We hear about all these wonderful capabilities that the system has, but we don't see them because there's nobody to show us how.

There's something very wrong in an organization that size that would roll out a major upgrade to customers and give them supporting documentation that was 50 percent outdated. In fact, I talked to some people who said they never even knew about the upgrade until they got a confusing screen on Monday morning!

Well, guys [summarizing a conversation he had with the fire-fighting team from our client], this is, unfortunately, part of the way we manage our business. We haven't found a better way of doing it, and we're not going to change how we work just to make it easier on your system.

Make us more productive than we are today. To me, its through technology.

Unless you stay on top of it with these types of vendors, they won't deliver on their own—they need someone to push them a little bit. And I've never seen an exception to that.

We might outsource our whole operation. There's a lot in this arena. You can see the bonuses for going with an outsourcing company...the bottom line. They come in and tell you they can do it cheaper, and they probably can.

After all the individual presentations were made, the video of customer comments was shown. By this point the group was tired and somber. Members had absorbed, discussed, denied, argued, and finally reached consensus on the information. It was an intense session. The voice of the customer was amplified and understood.

Here is the group's summary of the customer's voice:

Good News

- There was a huge opportunity for the Professional Services solutions.
- There was strong evidence that customers would pay favorable prices.
- No other supplier was yet filling the need for Professional Services.

Bad News

- The customers didn't feel that our client had the expertise they wanted; they were right.
- Several key decision makers were not happy with the current hardware or services provide by our client. If their underlying needs weren't addressed, word of mouth would sour a number of relationships.

FIGURE 6–3
Assess Business Issues

---

1. Review strategic documents
2. Interview senior management
3. Talk to outside experts

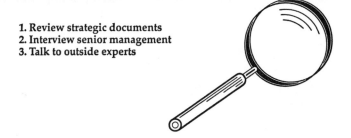

Next Steps

- The appropriate personnel were immediately informed about the customer dissatisfaction issues, and plans to close the feedback loop were developed.
- All top management were exposed to the findings.
- Customers that participated in the discovery research were presented the findings in account reviews.
- A "new" Professional Services plan was built to focus on obtaining the right expertise and fine-tuning and shortening the list of accounts to pursue.

Companies involved in the transition to Professional Services find that amplifying the voice of the customer is critical both to their ability to motivate the organization to change and to develop the correct set of solutions.

ASSESSING BUSINESS ISSUES

The Professional Services strategy must align with the overall business focus and take advantage of pressing issues and trends in the business environment. This means that the leader of the Professional Services transition project team must have a crystal clear understanding of the identified challenges, opportunities, and initiatives of senior management.

Figure 6–3 displays the three steps to assessing business issues. Assessing business issues starts with reviewing the strategic documents of the business. A careful analysis of strategic and operational plans and reports lets you get beyond the slogans and fluff of annual reports, PR bulletins, and internal employee publications. It is important to see not only what is stated but what is funded and monitored. This provides the basis on which to talk with executives.

Next, transition team members should actively seek time to personally interview senior management. A similar questioning approach as outlined in amplifying the voice of the customer should be used. Not only should the critical business issues be identified but also it should be understood why these issues are so important.

The questioning can be positioned like this. "Mr. Big Shot, I am excited about leading our new initiative into Professional Services. Although it will be challenging, the risks seem well worth the potential rewards. To make sure that my plans align with your priorities, I'd like to ask you a few questions. So that I can concentrate on what you're saying, I'd like to tape this conversation just for my own use."

In most cases executives respond very favorably to this approach. Some of the questions to ask include these: What issues keep you up at night? What is your biggest priority? Where do you see the holes in existing plans? The term *Professional Services* means different things to different people. Can you tell me how you define it? What role do you see Professional Services playing in the big picture? What recommendations do you have for me as I build the Professional Services organization? What questions do you have?

These meetings also give the transition team member a chance to position Professional Services in a way that aligns with senior management's thinking. This approach helps to educate senior management members and strengthen their commitment to Professional Services. The more senior management members know about Professional Services, the greater their buy in.

The third step is to talk to outside experts. There are almost always university academics or industry consultants who can give a fresh perspective on industry issues, trends, and specific challenges of competitors. Their insights can be a good reality check to the sometimes slanted view of company executives.

Develop a set of good questions and follow an approach similar to the one outlined earlier.

BUSINESS ISSUES EXAMPLE

Not doing your homework has its consequences. Here is an example of the potential impact of *not* assessing business issues.

An office systems client of ours was publicly professing (and funding) a campaign to offer its customers Professional Services through its distribution network. Training was being implemented, brochures were being sent, and a lot of energy and money were being spent.

The vice president of distribution wanted to build a consulting capability in line with the definition and description of Professional Services outlined in this book. He saw this as a way to truly differentiate the company in the marketplace.

The president *talked* about Professional Services as well. Every conversation and speech were peppered with references to providing the ultimate in Professional Services. However, what the president really *meant* when he said Professional Services was providing services professionally—and to him that meant making sure that all the service techs wore ties and had clean vehicles. When this difference finally surfaced at a quarterly review session, funding for Professional Services was quietly dropped and so was the vice president.

Assessing business issues is not lengthy or difficult. However, it is an important step in discovery that should not be overlooked.

A third element of discovery research analyzes star field performers. The concept is that top performers do things differently than average performers. Once you understand those differences, you can create a capability profile to use for hiring and evaluation. By understanding those differences, you can build custom training and developmental activities to improve the performance of your people. Depending on the situation, it sometimes makes sense to analyze star performers early in the transition project. In most situations, however, it makes the most sense to do this step as a part of the achievement phase. Analyzing star performers will be discussed in depth in Chapter Eight.

The discovery outcomes of amplifying the voice of the customer, and assessing business issues include the following:

- Facts based on customer and field reality—not internal guesses.
- In-depth understanding of key customer expectations, how well you meet them, and how you compare with the competition.
- Identification of critical customer issues.
- Benchmarks to measure progress.
- Motivational findings with the power to accelerate the transition to Professional Services.

Discovery lays the basis for moving into the future. Once discovery is completed, it is time to move on to blueprinting. Chapter Seven describes the blueprinting phase of the Professional Services transition project.

Chapter Seven

Phase 2: Blueprinting

Blueprinting Rationale
Blueprinting Session Guidelines
The Blueprint
Blueprint Benefits
Transition Project Plan

T he Professional Services transition project team and other key organizational players must now struggle with the information gathered during the discovery phase. The team must work together to develop a new and motivational direction based on areas of excellence and opportunity. Blueprinting helps create a new Professional Services strategy and mindset. The blueprinting phase provides the basic philosophical structure that initiates and accelerates culture formation.

To begin, we will discuss the need for blueprinting followed by an examination of the guidelines for effective blueprinting sessions. Next, we will give some examples of the benefits of blueprinting. Finally, we will discuss the transition project plan.

BLUEPRINTING RATIONALE

In our consulting work we are often challenged with the questions, Why Blueprinting? Why not eliminate this phase of the transition project and cut down on project expense? The feeling is that putting together a blueprint is nice but certainly not necessary. There is usually that same "just do it" attitude as discussed in Chapter Five. However, if we remember the Professional Services transition force field analysis, many forces are involved in the transition to Professional Services. Key people must be sold on making sometimes rather dramatic changes.

Blueprinting is a mechanism to leverage the positive transition forces and minimize the negative ones. It helps people with different issues, priorities, and viewpoints reach common ground. Blueprinting provides a forum for key people to challenge both the status quo and proposed change. It creates a positive environment that leads to consensus[1] and commitment.

The blueprint is the guiding force of the Professional Services organization. It *is* the strategy. It represents the rational "what" and "how" of the business along with the emotional "why."

Like the 10 commandments of Christianity and Judaism, a blueprint defines the expectations of how people should act. Whenever a member of the team faces a tough decision, the question should always be: What does our blueprint tell us to do? If there is such a thing as a sacred document in business, this is it.

The consequences of avoiding the blueprinting phase can be severe. We had worked with a fast-growing manufacturer of food products on a large-scale discovery project. The findings brought out potentially major organizational implications, especially for the sales organization. From the customers' eyes, our client no longer held a product quality advantage. Customers felt the premium price asked for by our client was no longer justified. Customers were begging for "consulting support" in everything from merchandising to training personnel.

The executive team was in a hurry to put out the fires surfaced by the research. They turned down the recommendation to bring key people from different departments together in a blueprinting session to thrash out the problems, struggle with possible solutions, and come to common agreement. Instead, the executive group made sweeping changes that affected most of the organization with a special impact on the sales force. In addition, the vice

---

1 Blueprinting is not a process of decision making by vote. There are significant differences between consensus-based decisions and "democratic" decisions. Consensus occurs when, after much discussion and debate, a decision is reached that, though everyone may not love it, they can live with it and act on it. Decisions made on the basis of voting often polarize participants and give the "losers" the motivation to undermine the decision.

president of sales used the discovery information to beat up certain individuals and justify changes he wanted to make.

Instead of building consensus and motivation around the voice of the customer, the organization had no team buy in, only resistance, to the changes. Morale plummeted, turnover increased, and most of the potential power of the information was forever lost.

The power of discovery is lost unless the insights gained are acted on. Blueprinting is the vital phase in the transition to Professional Services that brings discovery to action. Blueprinting must not be avoided.

BLUEPRINTING SESSION GUIDELINES

The blueprint is usually developed in a two- to four-day session consisting of the Professional Services transition project team and other key stakeholders. Depending on the situation, the group size may vary from 8 to 50 or more.[2] Experience shows that following these guidelines greatly impacts the chances of success.

Prepare Senior Management

Prepare senior management ahead of time. The top people present at the session must be fully aware of the probable and potential outcomes of such a session. Whatever boundaries need to be set, such as the availability of resources, size of budgets, or decision-making limits, senior management should establish them prior to the blueprinting session.

The roles and responsibilities of senior management must also be agreed on prior to the session. To have a successful session, the leadership must be in the role of group member with equal status to all other participants. The only exception to this is when situations arise for which Senior management can provide special knowledge or in areas for which boundaries need to be clarified.

---

[2] Group size is much less important than clearly defining the constraints, expectations, and required outputs up front. The facilitator must also manage the group's time firmly. See M Weisbord (1992). *Discovering Common Ground*. San Francisco: Berrett-Koehler Publishers.

Use Outside Facilitators

Blueprinting sessions are usually passionate events in which individuals with different ideas first challenge one another before finally coming together to reach consensus. This is one area in which you absolutely must use outside resources unless there is an internal consultant that you want to fire after the session bombs. The issues are too controversial and the emotions too hot for someone inside the organization to handle. It isn't fair to the inside consultant or to the organization to use.

Outside expertise adds a lot to the power of the session by helping guide the strong emotions to positive practical results while avoiding the political squabbles that occur in a natural environment. The outside facilitators must not only be good at process but also must understand the overall Professional Services objectives and the issues involved in this unique transition.

Allow Enough Time

Figure out how long you feel it should take and add one more day. It is guaranteed that very important issues will come up that must be addressed and that cannot be planned for. This session is too critical to rush to finish. Allocate enough time. An absolute minimum of two days is needed and usually three or four are appropriate, depending on group size and the complexity of the issues.

Get Away

Get as far away from the physical structure of the business as you can afford. The more removed and rustic the better. Keep the session highly casual. Try to ban phones, faxes, and computers.

Plan Carefully

Give careful thought to the process and methods used during the blueprinting. The session must be orchestrated in such a way to openly confront tough issues, examine personal beliefs, be open to a diversity of different views of the world, make solid decisions, gain consensus, and make people feel willing to contribute. This is challenging work.

FIGURE 7–1
Blueprint Example

Fundamental Values	Vision	Goals	Focus
Customer: The voice of the customer will be the foundation for our success. **Teamwork:** we expect active participation from all team members. **Integrity:** we promise to treat all our stakeholders with respect and openness. **Fun:** Life is short—we commit to working only with people and projects we enjoy.	Our purpose is to integrate information systems so that customers are better informed and more productive. We envision being recognized in our market as the global leaders in systems integration and major contributors to improved worldwide communications.	Maintain high levels of team satisfaction (minimum 4.0 on 5 point scale) Maintain high levels of client satisfaction (minimum 4.0 on 5 point scale) Grow business 20% per year Generate 25% international business Donate one week per person per year to worthy causes Benefit mankind	**Core competency:** Systems integration **Product:** Process reengineering **Customers:** Business information technology leaders **Market:** Fortune 1000 financial services and pharmaceutical businesses

Outdoor experiential exercises should be considered. "Tree-hugging" as a stand-alone exercise has limited value. It has been our experience, however, that the right type of outdoor activities can be a powerful complement to the session.

Be Flexible

Blueprinting is a dynamic, emotional process. Be ready and open to change direction from the planned agenda to address important issues the group identifies.

THE BLUEPRINT

The blueprint should be succinct, no more than one page in length. Our experience suggests that four categories should be part of the blueprint: fundamental values, vision, goals, and focus. Figure 7–1 displays an example of a Professional Services organization's blueprint.

Fundamental Values: The Organization's Conscience that Creates a Touchstone for Decision Making

Fundamental values were discussed in Chapter Two. These values represent the beliefs and principles on which the Professional Services organization is run. Fundamental values act as the organization's conscience that creates a touchstone for decision making. To be effective, members of the Professional Services team must be able to solve problems and make decisions at the point of customer contact. Stated, shared, believed, and reinforced, fundamental values give the Professional Services team members the boundaries, direction, and motivation to "do what's best" in virtually any situation.

For example, a Professional Services organization that had fun as a fundamental value chose not to go after the largest account in a targeted market. Although there was a very large financial incentive to get this business, the Professional Services team members felt that people from the account were stuffy, overly conservative, and boring. After an intense debate, the account was dropped from the prospect list.

Vision: A Vivid Picture of Where the Organization Must Go, What It Must Become, and How It Will Get There

The vision should guide and inspire the Professional Services organization around a common dream. The vision represents a future state that people can get excited about and strive to achieve. The most powerful visions (often audacious statements) are those that motivate people to achieve and go beyond "normal" ways of doing things. The vision must align with the fundamental values. Effective visions also contain an explanation of the mission, or what the organization does.

The "vision thing" has received a fair amount of bad press the last few years. Much of it is surely deserved. Some organizations have created visions just because their top management read that it was important to have a vision statement. No basis was made based on customer needs or business trends. They dutifully hired consultants, wordsmithed a glowing document, added it to all their brochures, announced it in the annual report, and sent every employee an oak-framed copy with instructions to hang it in their workplace. Mission accomplished—a vision statement in place just like all the other "excellent" companies have. If that is the end of it, then it should be the object of scorn. Unless a vision is continuously shared, discussed, reinforced, and lived, it has no power. It becomes just another relic in the basement.

Goals: Clear, Achievable, Measurable, and Motivational PS Priorities

Goals are the broad targets against which the organization must be measured. The vision is the oasis at the end of the journey, and the goals are the milestones along the way. Blueprint goals should be few in number (no more than five or six) yet should reflect the priorities of the Professional Services organization in ways that can easily be tracked.

We recommend that there be at least one goal reflecting some aspect of customer satisfaction, one on team satisfaction, one on innovation, and no more than two reflecting financial performance. Goals reflecting the world-class standing of the core competency (discussed in the next section) and broader social goals should be considered. The goals should be measurable, achievable, motivational, and easily understood by all stakeholders. Of course, they must align with both the vision and the values.

Focus: Identification of the Core Competency, High-Priority Customers, Markets, and Products

The focus determines the core competency of the business, the types of knowledge products the Professional Services organization will offer, the customers that will be targeted, and the markets that will be sought. The more specific the focus can be defined, the better.

Determining the focus represents one of the most challenging parts of blueprinting. Although everyone "knows" that the most effective organizations are highly focused, few organizations have the discipline to actually do it. Focus is the area on which personal biases come in to play and "logic" is severely challenged. Everyone has his or her own ideas as to which products, customers, and markets ought to be pursued. The values, vision, and goals help shape the focus, and the information gathered during discovery adds the necessary reality check when personal feelings come into play.

Focus is built around the concept of core competency.[3] Core competency states that an organization can be truly "world class" (*world class* means better than anyone else on the globe, not in your local area or industry) in only one area. The following are necessary to identify the core competency:

- Determine the one area on which you are now world class or the one area in which you should strive to be world class (many business proclaim to be world class, but few prove it).
- Devote your best thinking, target your best people, and provide maximum resources to support this one area of excellence.
- Work relentlessly to improve this one area.

To support the maximization of the core competency, the following should be accomplished:

- Determine the *minimum* levels of performance needed in *all* other areas of the business.
- Outsource as many of these functions, capabilities, and services as you can possibly stand.
- Provide the minimum level of resources necessary to support the noncore competency areas.
- Relentlessly manage the noncore competency areas (including those outsourced) to improve efficiencies, lower costs, and avoid taking up the organization's time and energy.

This "minimization" is not an easy concept to swallow. Imagine the former functional head of manufacturing who is told that the core competency of the business is systems integration and that manufacturing will now take a secondary role in the business.

The core competency drives the selection of products, customers, and markets. In a Professional Services organization, the concept of core competency is very important. If you really aren't

---

3 Prahalad, C K, and G Havel (1990). The core competence of the corporation. *Harvard Business Review*, 68 (3), 79–91.

world class in the knowledge solutions you provide, why should the customer even give you the time of day?

These four elements, fundamental values, vision, goals, and focus make up the blueprint. Linked together, they form the strategy of the Professional Services organization.

BLUEPRINT BENEFITS

The blueprint has a number of benefits, including the following.

Stakeholder Buy In

The most important value of the blueprint is to accelerate the buy in of stakeholders to the Professional Services transition. Since the blueprint was formed by a cross-section of people in the organization, they take ownership in the product of their work and sell the value to their peers.

Recruitment and Selection Tool

The blueprint succinctly states in motivational terms the who—how—why of the organization. It spells out the criteria needed to be a part of the team along with persuasive reasons for the recruit to want to join up. Team members should be selected and evaluated based on their alignment and commitment to the blueprint.

For example, one Professional Services organization lists all the fundamental values, vision, goals, and focus of their business along the left-hand side of a form. Candidates are listed across the top, forming a matrix. Each candidate is scored on how well the interviewers believe that he or she align with each element of the blueprint. This organization knows that knowledge and skills are not enough and utilizes the power of its blueprint.

Account Qualification

Along with the key success factors discussed in Chapter Three, the blueprint serves as an excellent guide to qualify accounts. the blueprint should be presented and discussed with all prospects. Accounts that don't align with the fundamental values, vision, goals, and focus may not be good candidates for business partnership. Areas of differences should be discussed and weighed before partnering or major business commitments are made.

Marketing Tool

The blueprint is also a marvelous marketing tool. It is our experience that most people are proud of a well-written blueprint. PS team members will "show off" and sell the PS organization to customers, prospects, potential employees, family, and friends. It is an excellent word-of-mouth promotional tool as discussed in Chapter Three.

Financial Return

It is worth the effort to create and nurture a blueprint for the Professional Services organization for one other pragmatic reason. **"Visionary companies" have outperformed average companies by a factor of 50 to 1 over the last several decades.**[4] Need anything else be said?

With the blueprint completed, the participants of the blueprinting session turn their energies to the transition project plan.

TRANSITION PROJECT PLAN

The purpose of the transition project plan is to get the new Professional Services organization up and running as quickly and effectively as possible. The transition project plan was started earlier at the time the decision was made to make the transition to Professional Services. At the blueprinting session, substance will be added to the transition project plan, and open discussion will speed its implementation.

The transition project plan includes these elements: project definition, objectives, stakeholder analysis, force field analysis, and

---

4 Quinn, J B (1992). *Intelligent enterprise: A knowledge and service based paradigm for industry.* New York: Free Press, p. 258, citing an article in *The Economist* (November 9, 1991), p. 89.

critical tasks. All participants of the blueprinting session work together to build the plan and map out responsibilities.

Project Definition

The project definition establishes the scope and the major inputs and outputs of the project. Inputs to the plan are information coming from the discovery phase, the professional services transition force field analysis, the blueprint, and the knowledge and experience of the participants. The final output, or product, of this project will be the up-and-running Professional Services organization including the three main elements of products, processes, and people.

Objectives

Just like the blueprint, the objectives of the transition project plan must be clear, achievable, measurable, and motivational. In addition, they should include the dimensions of quality, time, and budget. Objectives become the benchmarks for tracking project implementation success.

Stakeholder Analysis

Stakeholders are people who have a stake (something to gain or lose) in the implementation and the outcome of the transition project plan. Every important individual should be analyzed to consider his or her role in the accomplishment of the plan, his or her business and personal issues, and his or her personality.

Stakeholders must see the value of Professional Services to them if they are to support, or at least not hinder, implementation. This is an absolutely vital element of the plan. Realistically, there are probably 12 to 50 important stakeholders involved in the transition to Professional Services. Once the role, issues, and personality are determined, actions must be decided on to inform and influence each stakeholder. Chapter Three provides an example of a stakeholder analysis used in a selling situation. Chapter Nine provides more detail on using the stakeholder analysis and provides an example used during the transition process.

Force Field Analysis

The Professional Services force field analysis created at the beginning of the transition project (see Chapter Five) is now modified based on the new information that has been generated. The purpose of the force field is the same—to identify all the forces that can either help or hinder project success.

Critical Tasks

During the blueprinting session, it is important to first identify the most important tasks, define their scope, and assign key players. The information required to provide the level of detail needed is probably not available, nor is the time.

Experience shows that the critical transition tasks to be addressed include managing relationships, developing processes, developing products, developing people, and managing risk and opportunity. Figure 7–2 displays these critical tasks of the Professional Services transition project plan.

Manage Relationships. Stakeholders influence the success of the project, and the team's relationship with the stakeholders impacts their attitude and actions. Well-thought-out steps must occur early on and throughout the plan to sell the Professional Services idea and to educate and convince the stakeholders of the value of Professional Services to them personally. Again, Chapter Nine will address how this critical task is handled.

Develop Processes. Processes need to be developed, objectives set, requirements identified, and so on. Chapter Eight will address these issues. At the blueprinting session, it is important to review the concept of core processes with the group and get their buy in to the concept. From there, a team will be tasked with fleshing out the details.

FIGURE 7–2
Professional Services Transition Project Plan

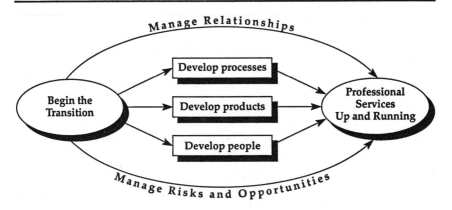

Develop Products. The product of Professional Services is knowledge. To make it easier for customers to buy Professional Services, the products must be packaged in a simple, straightforward way. The three categories of Professional Services products are training, process reengineering, and outsourcing.

Pricing is a major consideration in developing products, and Professional Services can be priced one of three ways: time, project, or pay for performance.

There is not the time or energy available at the blueprinting session to develop the product(s) completely or to determine pricing. The blueprinting session should devote some time, however, to assigning a team to work on this critical task, and to developing a timeline. Chapter Eight will address product and pricing.

DEVELOP PEOPLE

High-quality people are needed to effectively implement Professional Services. The capabilities needed to market, qualify, sell, and consult must be determined. Then the decision must be made as to whether to hire new personnel, develop existing performers, or utilize outside specialists. Chapter Eight will discuss this important issue further. Again, a critical task team will need to address this assignment.

Manage risks and opportunities. Numerous risks and opportunities will surface during the transition project. Many have already been identified through the stakeholder analysis and the force field. It is up to the transition project team to anticipate and minimize risks while developing and leveraging opportunities. Chapter Nine will discuss this critical task.

All of these critical tasks must be addressed in the transition to Professional Services. Special situations may warrant assigning other teams to deal with special issues and opportunities. All critical tasks need to have teams assigned with a designated leader, rough marching orders in place, and established timelines to track progress. With the completion of the critical task assignments, the blueprinting session is completed.

Blueprinting is a vital phase of the transition to Professional Services. It builds the blueprint of the new Professional Services organization and it provides the broad project plan framework to make things happen. Properly implemented, the outcomes include the following:

- High-quality team decisions that focus on critical PS priorities.
- Succinct, measurable blueprint with transition project plan in place.
- Establishment of the value of change.
- Participants with the ownership and motivation to make things happen.

Blueprinting sets the stage and provides the momentum for the successful accomplishment of the achievement phase.

Chapter Eight

Phase 3: Achievement

Develop Processes
Effective Processes
Develop Process Action Steps
Develop Products
Professional Services Pricing Issues
Pricing Maxims
Pricing Strategies
Product Design
Develop People
High-Impact Training
Continuous Learning

T he blueprinting session provides participants the vision and motivation to begin the long transition journey. With the Professional Services transition project plan having been bought into by the blueprinting group and blessed by senior management, the critical tasks of the transition plan must be developed, funded, and effectively executed.

The leader of each critical task team should follow the project management process outlined in Chapter Seven. It is important to note that each critical task should be planned and executed by a team that is knowledgeable of the activities, motivated to improve them, and has the time and resources to deliver.

It is up to the transition project leader to continually monitor critical task progress to meet the overall objectives of the transition project. This is detailed in Chapter Nine.

Depending on the situation, there may be numerous critical tasks to execute. Our experience shows, however, that the critical tasks described in Chapter Seven—develop processes, develop products, and develop people—must be implemented in any transition project. Implementation of these critical tasks is the achievement phase of the transition project. When the company has completed the achievement phase, it has an effectively functioning, dynamically stable Professional Services capability.

DEVELOP PROCESSES

The popular management literature is full of theory and stories demonstrating the fact that streamlining business processes can yield dramatic improvement of business performance. Whether called *process improvement*, *process management*, or *process reengineering*, the principles are the same. Many books have been written specifically on this subject, and we will not replow well-furrowed ground here.

The purpose here is to briefly overview the concepts that guide the improvement of any process and more important, to call the reader's attention to the fact that for Professional Services, many processes must be engineered for the first time. Our consulting experience suggests that for Professional Services, creating new processes and creating strong delivery teams is actually more important than the classic process streamlining approach of eliminating nonvalue-added steps and reducing headcount.

Regardless of whether engineering or reengineering processes, the characteristics of effective processes remain constant.

EFFECTIVE PROCESSES

Customer Value

Effective processes maximize customer value, minimize business requirements, and eliminate waste (see Chapter Three for more details).

Performance Goals

Goals should clearly specify the quality of process outputs, the cycle time of the process, and the associated costs. Measures of past performance should serve as benchmarks on which to build improvement. When benchmarks cannot be established up front, they should be developed quickly. When engineering new processes, team members will find that evaluating the process goals of world-class organizations is the best place to start.

Clearly Understood Procedures

Step-by-step procedures must be documented and communicated to all process participants. Procedures should be simple, specific, and accessible to all employees. When possible, the procedures should be supported by paper and pencil or electronic aids that guide accomplishment and assure quality.

Ownership

Every core process should have an "owner" with both the responsibility and the authority for the performance of the overall process. The process owner should be evaluated and rewarded on process performance. In addition, key activities within the processes should be owned, evaluated, and supported.

Simplicity

Processes should continually be monitored with the constant intent of trying to eliminate waste and simplify work flow. Alternative approaches should regularly be evaluated.

These five characteristics represent the basis for effective, efficient, and adaptive processes. These characteristics are a guide for the critical task team assigned to develop Professional Services processes.

DEVELOP PROCESSES ACTION STEPS

There are four action steps to developing Professional Services processes. The broad parameters are listed below for the critical task team to follow.

1. *Envision the ideal process.* Using the four core processes discussed in Chapter Three and the characteristics of effective processes as a touchstone, brainstorm concerning the way that

Professional Services *should* work at your company. Set aside the current organizational constraints and work from a blank sheet of paper. For the moment, forget about "how things are done around here."

It is often highly advantageous to search out examples of outrageous success in other companies in other industries. Determine the processes and activities inside them that make them so successful.

As the group works to create the ideal processes, visually display your work. Put each critical activity on note cards and attach them to the wall in sequence. Flowcharting[1] is easy and the preferred tool to map processes. Also estimate the cycle time and the activity time for each process and each process activity. Estimate the cost of peoples' time and color code the activities as to whether they create customer value, meet a business requirement, or add waste.

For example, imagine that you and your critical task team are working on the qualifying process. Brainstorming ideas, the team determines the ideal qualifying process. Figure 8–1 displays this ideal process.

This ideal qualifying process, has just three key activities. The suspect phones, the receptionist qualifies and, depending on his or her decision, either sets an appointment with a salesperson or asks for a referral.

Activity time is the time that each activity actually takes to complete. Cycle time includes the activity time *and* the time lag that occurs between activities. In this ideal scenario, each activity immediately follows the other so that activity time and cycle time are identical, each taking one hour total.

After reviewing the ideal process, the team is quite satisfied with the results: only three activities, taking only one hour, performed by only one person, each activity creating customer value, at a cost of only $30 to qualify an account. The critical task team posts the ideal qualifying process on the wall and vows to try to emulate it.

2. *Map the existing process.* The second step returns to reality. Map out, one at a time, each activity from input to output. Once you have identified what you *think* occurs, find out what *actually* hap-

---

[1] Harrington, H J (1991). *Business process improvement.* New York: McGraw-Hill, especially pp. 86–113.

FIGURE 8–1
The Ideal Qualifying Process

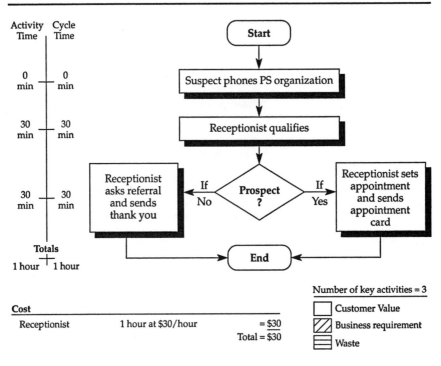

pens. Physically walking through the process is necessary to accurately determine the existing steps. Use existing data to confirm what you find and establish existing levels of performance. As in step 1, flow chart the processes and display pertinent information.

Returning to the qualifying process example, the team addresses the existing process. In this case, since Professional Services is new, members decide to examine how qualifying is done in the traditional side of their business. Team members talk to personnel in marketing and sales to discover the steps. They sit in with different people during the existing qualifying activities to learn what actually happens. What they find is pretty amazing. Figure 8–2 displays the existing qualifying process for the traditional business as the task team mapped it out.

FIGURE 8–2
The Existing Qualifying Process

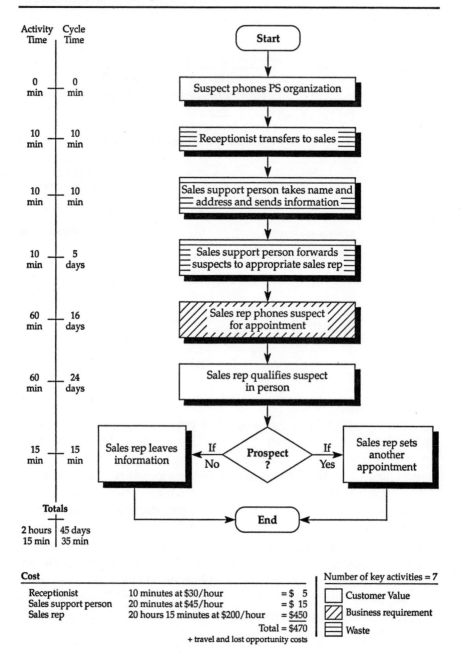

Activity Time	Cycle Time		
		Start	
0 min	0 min	Suspect phones PS organization	
10 min	10 min	Receptionist transfers to sales	
10 min	10 min	Sales support person takes name and address and sends information	
10 min	5 days	Sales support person forwards suspects to appropriate sales rep	
60 min	16 days	Sales rep phones suspect for appointment	
60 min	24 days	Sales rep qualifies suspect in person	
15 min	15 min	Sales rep leaves information — If No — Prospect? — If Yes — Sales rep sets another appointment	

Totals

2 hours 15 min | 45 days 35 min

End

Cost

Receptionist	10 minutes at $30/hour	= $ 5
Sales support person	20 minutes at $45/hour	= $ 15
Sales rep	20 hours 15 minutes at $200/hour	= $450
	Total =	$470

+ travel and lost opportunity costs

Number of key activities = 7

☐ Customer Value
▨ Business requirement
▤ Waste

The head of sales stated that qualifying was extremely important. All accounts that phoned in were expected to talk with a "real live" salesperson. What was happening, though, was that the salespeople were seldom in the office. The sales support person was taking about 75 percent of all incoming suspect calls. Being always pressed for time, the standard approach was to ask why they called; take their name, address, and phone number; send out a standard promotional brochure; and say that a salesperson would be calling them back.

The sales support person would then forward the suspect's information on to the respective salesperson. To be "efficient," the sales support person passed this information on only once a week or so, so the actual activity time of forwarding the information took about 10 minutes while the cycle time for this activity took an average of five days.

The sales reps were required to call all suspects and set up as many appointments as possible. They were directed not to try qualify on the phone because management believes that face-to-face qualifying leads to more sales.

Getting the appointment with the suspect was a real hassle for the salespeople, taking from three to six phone calls over several days' time. Usually the face-to-face appointment was scheduled two to four weeks out, so the time from the suspect's phone call to the company to the time of the face-to-face appointment was an average of 45 days!

During the appointment the sales representative qualified the account and set up another appointment if the account qualified. If the account was not a prospect, the salesperson left information and asked the account to call back if things changed.

This scenario has seven key activities involving three people. Four activities delivered customer value; three added waste. The total activity time was 2 hours and 45 minutes, but the cycle time was 45 days and 35 minutes. The time costs of the people involved was $470, not including travel or related expenses.

The team speculated that the *real* costs of qualifying this way were much higher. The salespeople could have been using their valuable (expensive) time much more effectively selling already qualified accounts. The team also speculated that the large time span from when the suspect phoned and when he or she talked to the salesperson was a big issue. Salespeople said that during that time, accounts often lost interest, found other solutions, or forgot why they called in the first place. Team members knew that they could improve on this performance.

3. *Create the new process.* The next step is to create the new process by evaluating the effectiveness and the rationale of the existing process performance and comparing it with the ideal. Display the maps of both the ideal and the existing process side by side on the wall. While reviewing the flow chart of the existing process, ask yourself the following questions:

Why is this activity being done?

How could this activity be done simpler, easier, faster?

How could this activity be error proofed?

How does this activity add value?

What would happen if this activity were eliminated altogether?

Again, map out the new process activities on cards and put them on the wall. Compare the new process against your ideal. Challenge *every* activity before including it in a process. Ask yourself these questions:

Can further simplifications or eliminations be made?

Do critical steps and linkages need to be added?

What is the result if an activity isn't included?

In the qualifying example, the critical task team created the new process map displayed in Figure 8–3.

When a suspect phones in, it is mandatory that the sales administrator take the call. The sales administrator will then qualify the suspect. If the suspect is qualified, the sales administrator sets an appointment and immediately sends the suspect an appointment reminder card. If the suspect does not qualify, he or she is asked for a referral and then immediately is sent a thank you letter. In either case, the sales administrator enters the information from the suspect call into the information system, which the respective salesperson (or anyone in the organization for that matter) can instantly access on the PC.

The task team is pleased with this new process map. There are only five process activities, three of which add customer value and

FIGURE 8–3
The New Qualifying Process

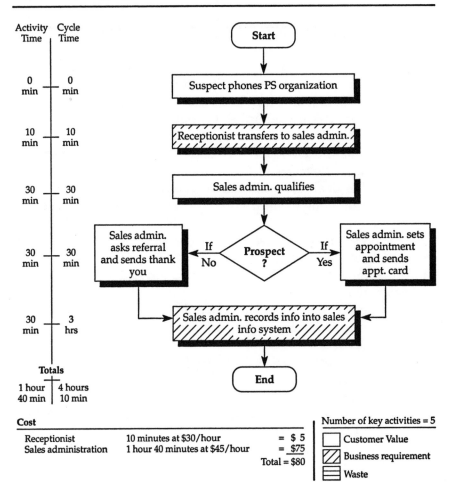

Activity Time	Cycle Time	

Cost

Receptionist	10 minutes at $30/hour	= $ 5
Sales administration	1 hour 40 minutes at $45/hour	= $75
		Total = $80

Number of key activities = 5

☐ Customer Value
▨ Business requirement
☰ Waste

two of which meet a business requirement. Only two people are involved in the key activities with activity time taking only 1 hour and 40 minutes and cycle time taking only 4 hours and 10 minutes. The cost of qualifying one account is only $80.

4. *Implement.* A very important part of developing processes is getting the buy in of key stakeholders. The same thoughtful stakeholder analysis discussed in Chapter Seven needs to take place

during this critical task. Many stakeholders will resist changing the status quo. They must see the benefits to the organization and what is in it for them personally before they will commit to implementing potentially radical change. Be sure that you can demonstrate how the new processes can increase revenue, decrease costs, and make everyone's working life better.

Once you have sold the team's recommendations, you have to deploy the Professional Services processes throughout the organization. A process owner must be determined and goals established. You or fellow team members will have to develop explanatory material and aids to train people in the new processes. The process should be translated into organizationally sanctioned procedures with clear responsibilities laid out.

In our qualifying example, a key success factor worksheet similar to the one discussed in Chapter Three was developed to maximize process quality. The sales administrator was to follow the format with every suspect. The identical format was built into the information system so that the organization had a common qualifying language.

The sales administrator was made the "owner" of the qualifying process and made responsible for coming up with performance goals and a set of procedures.

Developing processes and getting the necessary buy in to their use is a time-consuming and often challenging task. However, using the guidelines and following these four steps will lead to effective processes that maximize customer value, minimize business requirements, and eliminate waste.

Another critical task team looks at developing products.

DEVELOP PRODUCTS

The team charged with developing products must create a knowledge product that can profitably be sold to customers. Developing Professional Services products is a blending of in-depth knowledge of the customer, the technical expertise of the Professional Services organization, and the packaging know-how. The final knowledge product must be the correct blend of all three. Figure 8–4 demonstrates this graphically.

FIGURE 8–4
Developing Products

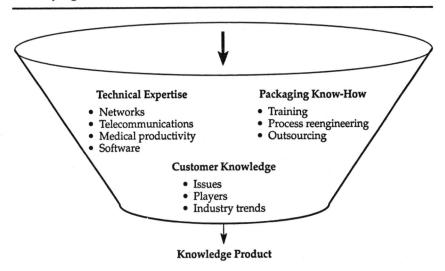

Knowledge Product

The most valuable technical expertise is that derived from the Professional Services core competency discussed in Chapter Seven. The in-depth knowledge of the customer comes from the discovery phase outlined in Chapter Six. The packaging know-how comes from areas such as adult learning, performance technology, and the quality movement.

The three product packages of Professional Services are training, process reengineering, and outsourcing. Each package possesses certain strengths and weaknesses. Each package addresses certain business issues but not others.

Training

Training bundles knowledge into a product that enhances the skills, knowledge, and mindset of individuals and teams to improve performance.

Later in this chapter a model for the creation of a training system for the Professional Services organization is discussed.

The critical task team for developing products must integrate these "training quality requirements" into its design and deployment if members hope to build an excellent training product for their Professional Services solution. If the training product is not of demonstrably high quality, the customer will go elsewhere for knowledge.

Process Reengineering

Process reengineering packages knowledge in a product that eliminates waste and speeds effective performance in specific customer functions or processes. Earlier in this chapter, the characteristics for effective processes were explained and the steps laid out that the Professional Services organization should take to engineer its own processes.

The critical task team must integrate these quality requirements into its design and deployment if task team members hope to build an excellent process reengineering package for their Professional Services.

Outsourcing

Outsourcing is a knowledge product that releases the customer from specific activities and responsibilities. Effective outsourcing lets the customer focus on its core competencies and not worry about the process/tasks/functions being outsourced.

The outsourcing product should be able to stand alone as a unique business. It is the task of the managers who run it to hire, train, and deploy the kind of people who will do the job effectively yet at the lowest cost. State-of-the-art productivity and quality tools must be consistently applied to ensure that the customer receives more value than it would have if it did it itself.

Another factor that must be considered before the product is designed is pricing.

PROFESSIONAL SERVICES PRICING ISSUES

Pricing the knowledge product is a complex challenge for most organizations transitioning to Professional Services. In many instances the Professional Services product is new to the market-place. There is no standard pricing that is already understood and "accepted" by the customer, so there is no similar pricing for the account to compare the relative value of your Professional Services against others.

Often the customer has received *similar sounding* services free. In this case there will probably be resistance to *any* price by the potential customer. In addition, many of the costs to design, build, staff, and deliver the product are not fully understood at this point. Because of these complexities, pricing principles, or maxims, are important in introducing the Professional Services product.

PRICING MAXIMS

The following are the maxims that guide pricing decisions.

1. *Value is what the customer says it is.* In Professional Services, value is derived from improving the customer's business performance resulting in increased revenue/margins and/or reduced costs.

2. *The value-to-price ratio drives buying behavior.* Customers purchase Professional Services when they believe that

   - The value received outweighs the costs incurred enough to warrant action.
   - They are confident in your ability to deliver.
   - Your value-to-price ratio is greater than competitive choices.

3. *Assume no relationship between cost and value.* See maxim 1.

4. *Value should be quantified.* The easier it is for the customer to see the value-to-price ratio in dollars and cents, the easier for it to justify the purchase.

5. *Costs must be quantified and constantly managed.* Costs should continually be driven down to maximize customer value and Professional Services profit.

6. *The customer should pay according to the value received.* Ideally, the more value, the more the customer should pay. No value—no pay.

If you cannot calculate value, follow the time-honored pricing formula outlined in Chapter Two:

Price = Cost + The margin desired by executive management – What you need to do to meet competition

When this is your pricing strategy, hope that the customer buys your Professional Services product on faith.

PRICING STRATEGIES

With these pricing maxims in mind, the product team can decide to price the Professional Services product in one of three ways: by time and materials, by the project, or pay for performance.

Time and Materials

Similar to the way lawyers and accountants charge for their services, the simplest way for the Professional Services organization to price is by actual time spent working on an assignment. Hourly or daily rates are set and agreed on. Time logs and expenses are kept. The customer is billed weekly or monthly for time and materials.

Many customers are reluctant, however, to agree to this approach until they have confidence in the value of the Professional Services. Pricing by time works best *after* a relationship and value have been established.

Project

Many customers prefer pricing based on a specific project. It allows them to budget more easily and to limit liability. It is easier for the customer to visualize the end result and thus weigh value versus price.

The downside is that very clear expectations must be set, yet often objectives are fuzzy in Professional Services. The risk to the

Professional Services organization is that many more hou₁₃ ⸺ be invested than planned to complete the project and keep the customer happy. We recommend starting with a small, easily defined project as the initial work with a new customer. This allows both organizations a chance to learn about each other before jumping into complex, ambiguous assignments.

Pay for Performance

Pay for performance is exactly what it states. The Professional Services organization is rewarded partly or entirely on the delivery of specific, measurable results. This is the ultimate in Professional Services—the customer gets the results he or she wants and the Professional Services organization is rewarded by receiving a share of the cost saving or new revenue generated.

Critical factors used to negotiate include the exact results agreed on, the specific commitment of both organizations and the procedures if the commitments are not fulfilled, the percentage of the savings/revenue involved, and the time frame. Trust must be established between both organizations before pay for performance is a viable option.

With knowledge product categories defined and pricing principles and strategies reviewed, it is time to design specific Professional Services products.

PRODUCT DESIGN

There are numerous, often complex, approaches to product design.[2] A review of these approaches is beyond the scope of this book. However, there are some guiding steps that apply very well

---

[2] Quality function deployment, particularly when category weighting techniques are added to it, is a powerful tool for product development. QFD aligns the voice of the customer with the capabilities of the organization and then builds product solutions and deployment strategies that are truly customer driven. It is important to note that most of the excellent texts in the area of product development apply to hard goods (S C Wheelwright and K B Clark (1992). *Revolutionizing product development: Quantum leaps in speed, efficiency, and quality.* New York: Free Press) or consumer services (J L Heskett, W E Sasser, and C W L Hart, (1990). *Service breakthroughs: Changing the rules of the game.* New York: Free Press), rather than the creation of the knowledge product of Professional Services.

in designing the knowledge products of Professional Services. Figure 8–5 displays a flow chart of the steps to product design.

The key is to examine the information available from the discovery and blueprinting phases and to look critically at what can work and then to test the idea and refine the results.

Along with processes and products, people must be developed.

DEVELOP PEOPLE

A question often asked is: Should I hire, train, or outsource people? Choosing the best answer is specific to your situation. Although many factors are involved in coming up with the correct answer, the most important are the sophistication of the customer and the product compared with the capabilities of your existing team. The existing team capabilities combined with their capacity to learn determines the best combination of training, hiring, or outsourcing personnel.

However, sometimes there is no choice. For political or financial reasons, internal people must be used. Experience provides a rough rule of thumb. For every 100 people in a traditional sales and service organization, 10 percent are already thinking and doing Professional Services–type activities. They need only a little direction and encouragement. Thirty percent will never successfully make the transition no matter how much money is spent or how much effort is expended. Frustration on everyone's part is the only outcome in trying to develop this group.

The middle 60 percent is where the greatest potential lies. With the proper training and development and the right management support system, this group can flourish—given enough time. Some organizations overcome these obstacles and quick-start Professional Services by outsourcing independent experts for a year or so while they grow their own people.

Chapter Four discusses the critical capabilities that a Professional Services team must possess and the performance system that is necessary to ensure that those skills are delivered. The critical task team should start with an assessment of the existing personnel slotted for the Professional Services organization to determine performance potential. The assessment should start by analyzing star performers. Here are those steps.

FIGURE 8–5
Steps to Product Design

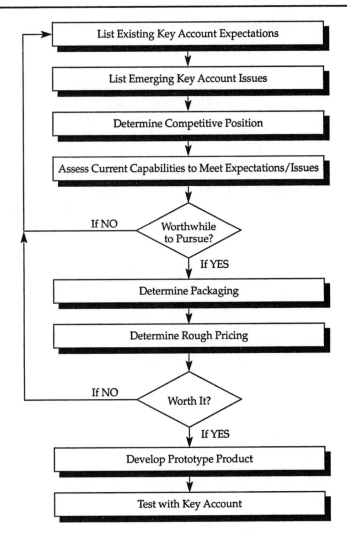

Analyze Star Performers

In every organization there is a handful of top performers, or stars, who perform exceedingly well in spite of poor plans, lack of tools, ill-focused measurement, and misguided management. This small group will be successful in spite of everything that gets in its way. This group does a few things differently than the rest because of unique knowledge, different skills, or special tools. They often have some unique insights, and involving them in the process helps gain their buy in to change and helps sell others in the organization who respect their capabilities.

1. *Select the best.* Top performers should be selected based on results. If Professional Services is new, there are still probably a few service and sales personnel whose natural inclination leans toward Professional Services. Usually star performers are easy to identify. Ask five people inside the organization who the best people are and the lists come back looking very similar. We recommend identifying two to three star performers and one to two average performers to analyze.

2. *Observe/interview.* People often don't do what they say they do, and star performers usually don't know why they do what they do. They have not had the opportunity or motivation to perform a critical self-analysis of their performance. That is why it is important to tag along on actual customer calls and observe star performers in their normal servicing/selling/consulting environment. After observation, the stars are interviewed to learn why they did what they did and why they didn't do other things. Sometimes they are asked to provide critical incidents or stories of different situations.

The same approach is followed in working with average performers. Observing and interviewing average performers helps identify and define the gaps between the stars and the normal performers.

Next, a group of three to seven star performers are brought together for one to two days to confirm key issues, determine star uniqueness, and define common star characteristics. Additional information gathered includes, information about what gets in the way of success and what ideas this elite group has to improve performance.

3. *Analyze data.* The data are then analyzed to determine the distinguishing behaviors—what makes stars to be stars? The output of analyzing star performers is a competency profile to be used as a guide for hiring, training, and outsourcing. The competency profile fleshes out the four critical capabilities discussed in Chap-

ter Four specific to individual needs of the Professional Services organization.

Under each of the four categories (selling skills, project management, technical knowledge, and business acumen), the specific tasks that must be performed are listed. There should be a completed competency profile for each of the four core processes. For example, Figure 8–6 displays a partially completed Professional Services competency profile for the selling core process.

4. *Compare current capabilities with required capabilities.* Next, it is time to take a look at current capabilities compared to requirements. Evaluate your company's current people resources based on the list of tasks. Score your people on the 1 to 5 scale from "doesn't meet requirements at all" to "totally meets requirements" for each task. Review the scores on the tasks to determine overall individual, group, and company capabilities. Review the results for specific areas of weakness and strength both at the task and capability level.

Remember that a high level of competence is not needed by each individual—it must just be resident in the team.

5. *Decide to hire, train, outsource, use or some combination.* Now the critical task team to develop people must assess the cost of hiring new people, training existing personnel, or outsourcing expertise to reach the needed competency in each of the four capabilities.

The following are some of the questions you will have to answer:

How important are the gaps identified?

How big are the gaps?

Could the gaps be filled with enough effort?

What type of training is most appropriate?

How easily can individuals outside of the organization who possess special expertise be contracted to participate on the team?

In searching for answers, the team should talk with internal and external experts on the cost vs. benefits of various strategies.

6. *Implement.* With plans to develop people in place, they must now be sold to the rest of the organization. The smart critical task team performs a stakeholder analysis to discover the roles, issues, and personalities of all stakeholders.

FIGURE 8–6
Professional Services Competency Profile

Core Process: Selling_____

Name: _____

	Doesn't Meet Requirements at All			Totally Meets Requirements
Selling Skills					
• Diagnose customer issues	1	2	3	4	5
• Develop customer urgency	1	2	3	4	5
• Negotiate fair projects	1	2	3	4	5
	1	2	3	4	5
	1	2	3	4	5
Project Management					
• Develop solid plans	1	2	3	4	5
• Manage stakeholders	1	2	3	4	5
• Manage problems	1	2	3	4	5
	1	2	3	4	5
	1	2	3	4	5
Technical Knowledge					
• Understanding systems integration	1	2	3	4	5
• Troubleshoot system errors	1	2	3	4	5
• Recommend technical fix	1	2	3	4	5
	1	2	3	4	5
	1	2	3	4	5
Business Acumen					
• Understand customer strategy	1	2	3	4	5
• Know functional business issues	1	2	3	4	5
• Understand TQM	1	2	3	4	5
	1	2	3	4	5
	1	2	3	4	5

FIGURE 8–7
High-Impact Training

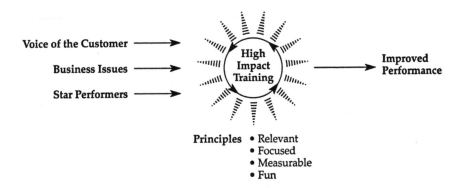

Voice of the Customer ⟶

Business Issues ⟶

Star Performers ⟶

High
Impact
Training

⟶ Improved
Performance

Principles • Relevant
           • Focused
           • Measurable
           • Fun

The team must be ready to address issues such as the cost and time necessary to hire new personnel, the question of buying versus building training,[3] the effect of recommendations on compensation costs, and commitments. Be sure that you can demonstrate how your solutions can increase revenue, decrease costs, and make everyone's working life better.

HIGH-IMPACT TRAINING

Our experience suggests that one of the vitally important solutions that your team will recommend will be training. Most companies transitioning to Professional Services have deficits in all four capabilities, with the most significant gap being in selling. People will need to be provided the right knowledge, skills, and tools to close that gap, and training is the appropriate answer.

We recommend a specific process to developing such training solutions that not only build the skills but also create the motivational buy in to those skills and deploy the management reinforce-

---

3 Though most sales and service organizations recognize the need to develop their people, efforts—particularly for service people—are all too often hurried, underfunded, and lack reinforcement. Our experience also suggests that off-the-shelf training is less than effective in the complex, organization specific environment of Professional Services.

ment to make the skills work. Figure 8–7 displays the process of high-impact training.

High-impact training is built on three inputs: the voice of the customer, the unique business issues of the organization, and the best practices of star performers. Select principles drive the development of the training system. The training is specific to your business customers so that participants immediately see the relevance to them. The training is focused on the "vital few" areas that the blueprint, the customer, and the star performers have shown are the most critical. The training is measurable so that performance improvement can be reinforced and tracked. Finally, the training is fun.

The end outcomes of this training system are Professional Services team members with improved competencies and the resulting improvements in performance.

CONTINUOUS LEARNING

Team members should learn not only in formal training sessions but also from the actions of their peers. Special efforts must be made to hold regular process/account/project review meetings. At these sessions, team members should share what is going on and what they have learned about working with the customer and with one another.

All Professional Services personnel should have ready access to all information resident in the organization. This allows personnel the opportunity to learn from the successes and failures of peers involved in previous projects.

Each team member should have his or her own personal development plan along with ample funding and time allocated to make it happen. Along with on-going reading in current areas of expertise, team members should spend a minimum of 10 to 15 days per year in some sort of personal development.

Finally, it is management's responsibility to make sure that expectations are clear, performers have necessary tools to do their job, interference is minimized, consequences are in place, feedback is quick and specific, and the rewards and recognition are appropriate to performance.

The achievement phase develops the products, processes, and people needed to deliver Professional Services. Strong planning, dedication, and action make the dream of blueprinting a reality.

Throughout achievement, tracking is in place to monitor progress, scan the environment for trouble, and continually adjust plans. Chapter Nine discusses the tracking phase.

Chapter Nine

Phase 4: Tracking

Manage Relationships
Manage Risks and Opportunities
Day-to-Day Tracking
Conclusion

O nce the Professional Services organization is up and running, the blueprint itself becomes the main vehicle for tracking the overall success of the organization. How well the business is accomplishing the fundamental values, vision, goals, and focus should be assessed on a regular basis.

During the transition phase, however, the only tracking that is a concern is how well the Professional Services transition project plan is being accomplished. The leader of each critical task team is responsible for tracking his or her respective critical task. Once the critical task team plans are approved, it is team members' responsibility to do what it takes to meet the objectives laid out in the critical task plan. However, the leader of the transition project plan has overall responsibility to bring the project in up to quality, on time, and within budget. The buck stops here.

One thing is certain in a project of this complexity, importance, and visibility: Issues will arise that have the potential to greatly impact the outcome of the project, either positively or negatively. The average project leader *reacts* to issues as they occur to minimize damage. The excellent project leader *anticipates* issues and leverages them to positively impact the project.

The excellent leader of the transition project continually manages relationships while managing risks and opportunities. Figure 9–1 highlights these two critical tasks of the transition project.

FIGURE 9–1
Manage Relationships and Manage Risks and Opportunities

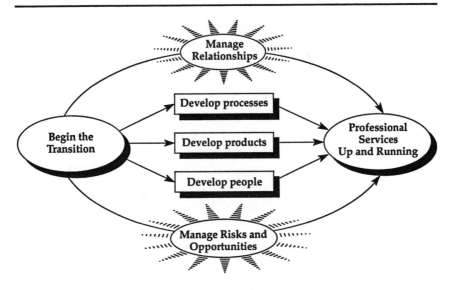

MANAGE RELATIONSHIPS

Almost every Professional Services transition project will have at least 20 stakeholders, including numerous people from the three broad categories identified in the force field analysis: senior management, customers, and the team. Senior management may include personnel from a number of different functions or even separate divisions within the company. The transition team will include outside consultants and possibly other experts borrowed from other parts of the business. Depending on the particular situation, customers may actively be involved in the transition project. Relationships with all key stakeholders must be created, improved, and managed.

Remember that by definition, a stakeholder has something to gain or to lose by the success or failure of the Professional Services transition project. *All* stakeholders need to be informed as to how the transition project meets their needs. There is a high probability that no matter how important Professional Services is to the future of the business or how much practical sense the project plan makes, certain stakeholders will resist the transition project.

This resistance may come in many forms. Certain stakeholders may be ambivalent to the project and thus not actively support it. Some will pay lip service to the importance of Professional Services while trying to undermine project success. A few will consciously and actively try to sabotage the project. This is a natural occurrence, and the project leader needs to openly understand this fact of organizational life and make plans to minimize damages.

The majority of stakeholders, however, will support the project once they see the value in it for them. Therefore, a critical factor in the success or failure of the transition project is the project leader's ability to communicate the value of the project to all key stakeholders in a way that meets their business and personal issues. This is the essence of managing relationships.

In the blueprinting session discussed in Chapter Eight, a stakeholder analysis was created listing all the main stakeholders, their roles in the transition project, both their personal and business issues, and their personality types. The stakeholder analysis is the main tool the project leader uses to help manage relationships. Figure 9–2 displays a typical stakeholder analysis (partially completed).

Here is the process for completing the stakeholder analysis. First the name of the stakeholder is listed under the left-hand column. Next, that person's role is listed. Stakeholders assume one of four roles due to position, special expertise, or area of interest. The four roles are decision maker, influencer, implementer, and coach. One person only has the power to stop the transition project with a single word. This person, often the chief executive, may be quite removed from the day-to-day activities of the transition. However, the true decision maker must be identified and continually sold on the value of Professional Services. Most stakeholders are influencers. Influencers have the ability to persuade other stakeholders for good or for ill. Implementers are the individuals who do the actual work. This includes most of the people on the project team. The last stakeholder role is the coach. The coach is unique because this person has special knowledge about other transition project stakeholders but doesn't have any vested business interest in the project. The coach wants the project leader to succeed because it is

FIGURE 9–2
Stakeholder Analysis

STAKEHOLDER ANALYSIS

Stakeholder	Role	Issues	Personality Type
	• Decision maker • Influencer • Implementer • Coach	• Business – Personal	• Dominant • Influencer • Steady • Compliance
Art W. President	Decision maker	• Business growth • Profitability – Look good to board	Dominant
Karen W. V.P. Sales	Influencer	• Declining margins • Sales cycle time – Keep job	Influencer
Jeff I. Int'l V.P. Service	Influencer	• Declining margins • Rising service costs – Hassle, job stress	Steady
Marilyn S. Dir. Marketing	Influencer	• Declining margins • New products – Appear leading edge	Steady
John A. V.P. Manufacturing	Influencer	• Slow product sales • Pressure on efficiencies – By the book	Compliance
Krystal H. Outside Consultant	Implementer	• Make Professional Services work – Save job	Steady
Alex S. Outside Consultant	Implementer	• Meet project objectives • Improve performance • Satisfy client – Gain future business	Dominant
Jan E. Dir. Finance	Coach	• Help business – Personal satisfaction helping project leader succeed	Influencer

the right thing to do. Coaches can be vital in helping cut through politics to find out what is really going on. The coach doesn't have to be a member of the business but could be an outside consultant, supplier, or customer that knows the organization, its players, and how they operate.

Next, both the business issues and personal issues are listed for each stakeholder. These are the problems, objectives, and needs that keep the stakeholder up at night. With a little thought and homework, business issues are usually readily identifiable. It is important to always consider the personal issues as well as the business issues. Although almost everyone wants to see the business succeed, if someone sees the transition as a personal threat to a possible promotion, loss of status, or potential loss of job, he or she will actively fight to stop it. By the same token, a person who sees it meeting his or her personal issues can be influenced to support the Professional Services transition project.

Next, estimate the personality type of the stakeholder. Numerous personality profile systems are available.[1] The personalities displayed in Figure 9–2 fall into one of four categories: dominant, influencer, steady, compliant. Individuals fall roughly into one of these four categories, and individuals with these categories have similar traits and behaviors.

The importance of the exercise, however, is not the ability to precisely peg a person as either a D, I, S, or C, but to look at the world through their eyes. They may have totally different perspectives on how to view the world. The project leader must understand and respect these differences of views and styles of working when planning how to manage relationships.

An understanding of each stakeholders's role, issues, and personality provides the information necessary to determine what actions the project leader should take. Questions to consider for each stakeholder include these:

What information does this stakeholder need to address these issues?

How should this information be communicated?

---

[1] Geier, J (1980). *Personal profile system*. Minneapolis, MN: Carlson Learning Co.

Who should communicate it?

When should communication take place?

If you don't know some of the information about a stakeholder, you better find out. Research the person to discover more about him or her. If the person has a critical role, consider interviewing, recording, and transcribing the conversation using the steps outlined in Chapter Six.

The stakeholder analysis calls for action to actively manage relationships through continuous communication. Communication might include formal presentations, project review sessions, one-on-one meetings, phone calls, newsletters, routing articles, or memos. The project leader will be the best person to communicate in some instances but not in others. A specific team member may have an existing relationship with a key stakeholder. Sometimes a consultant is the best person to communicate the rationale and benefits of the Professional Services transition to specific individuals.

Managing relationships starts the day the decision is made to transition to Professional Services and never stops until the Professional Services organization is up and running.

MANAGE RISKS AND OPPORTUNITIES

Risks and opportunities will occur throughout the life of the project. Contingency planning is the main tool to ensure that the critical task leaders and the leader of the Professional Services transition project team anticipate the future. This proactive planning minimizes risk and leverages opportunities. Figure 9–3 displays a partially completed contingency plan.

Contingency planning should start immediately on creation of the project. The contingency plan should be reviewed and updated regularly.

The first step is to identify all the important possible risks to the success of the project. One of two kinds of risks should be considered. The first risks have a high probability of occurring. The second type of risk has a low probability of occurring, but if one does arise, it will have a major impact on the project.

FIGURE 9–3
Contingency Plan

Risk/Opportunity	Probable Cause	Prevent/Minimize Risk Leverage/Create Opportunity
• Key person taken away	• Need expertise to put out fires	• Written commitment
• Cut/slow funding	• Business downturn (product sales)	• Tap other budgets
• A task team flounders	• Doesn't have right skills	• Provide project management training
• Crisis on old job	• Lack of personal attention	• Empower subordinate
• Takes more money than planned	• Poor planning	• Revisit budgets/reality check
• Competition launches new PS products	• Business need	• Involve key accounts early in process
• Customer requests help	• No one else helping	• Get customer to fund pilot
• Product development failure	• Not based on the voice of the customer	• Tap old funds—get key people
• Executive retreat	• Need good speakers	• Get on agenda
• Quarterly sales meeting	• Educate/motivate sales team	• Get on agenda

Figure 9–3 lists some common risks that almost all Professional Services transition projects will have. A key person will be taken away because senior management needs his or her special skills to put out some major fire. Funding may be slowed or cut because some key stakeholder wants to divert monies or there is a slowdown in the overall business. One of the critical task teams flounders because the leader lacks the skills or the time or isn't really committed to the task. The transition project leader may have a crisis on the old job and be diverted from the transition.

Once all the risks are identified, it is important to understand why they happen. The probable cause should be noted. Finally, ideas to eliminate or minimize risks should be brainstormed and the best solutions implemented.

The reason to identify potential problems is obvious, but the reason to identify opportunities is less so. The rationale for identifying opportunities is that, during the life of a project, fortuitous incidents occur:

- A large potential customer requests help with a problem that Professional Services can help solve.
- A product development failure has potentially freed up additional funds.

The transition project team must use these opportunities to leverage the visibility and speed the full implementation of Professional Services.

Other opportunities may not be so obvious. For example, senior management has an executive retreat every year to discuss the future of the business. The leader of the transition project might persuade the people organizing the retreat to include an outside expert (who happens to be on the Professional Services transition project team) on the program to talk about the business trends toward Professional Services.

Sales may have quarterly sales meetings. This may be an opportunity to start educating the sales organization about Professional Services, further assessing their willingness and capability...and to continue winning over sales allies.

The savvy Professional Services transition team member will have put together a sexy presentation and actively present it at every internal meeting they can. The transition team leader may convince an eager customer to help fund a Professional Services pilot to test out solutions. The key is to actively scan the environment to create opportunities.

The contingency plan is a powerful tool for the transition project leader. Properly used, it eliminates and minimizes risk while creating and leveraging opportunities.

DAY-TO-DAY TRACKING

The Professional Services transition project leader's office looks like the war room at Cheyenne Mountain. PERT charts and Gantt charts are stuck on the walls listing critical activities and timelines.

The stakeholder analysis and contingency plan are worn and frayed from review and constant changes.

Effective project leaders do a number of things to manage relationships, risks, and opportunities. They know that the old management adage that "you have to inspect what you expect" is true. They monitor all aspects of the transition project on a daily basis using the project plan as the main resource. They hold regular review meetings to discuss the progress of the critical tasks and the overall project. They schedule one-on-ones to meet with key stakeholders to influence action.

Tracking is the eyes and ears of the transition project's success.

Tracking tells the transition project team whether and how well it is meeting project goals. Tracking includes the following:

- Monitoring the transition project progress.
- Comparing planned results and activities to the actual occurrence.
- Revising the plan to bring the project in at quality, time, and budget expectations.

The tracking phase of the transition project starts the day the project becomes reality and continues throughout the transition. When the tracking phase is completed, all elements of the Professional Services transition project are up and running.

CONCLUSION

The Knowledge-Based Organization provides you with both the conceptual model of the fully functioning, high-performance Professional Services organization and the guidelines to create your own. Nevertheless, as discussed throughout the book, the transition to Professional Services is challenging.

This journey is fraught with pot holes, one-way streets, and missing road signs. It entails major changes in processes and products and often dramatic shifts in the skills, knowledge, and mindset of people, yet it is the only destination appropriate for many sales and service organizations.

Many businesses will start on the Professional Services super highway but get detoured and not complete the trip. Some will run out of gas, many will break down, while others will get detoured toward other points of interest. The transition to Professional Services requires a good road map, well-running equipment, commitment, and stamina.

Organizations that commit to a Professional Services strategy and follow the steps outlined in this book will reach their destination. The pay off for the hard work of Professional Services will be success for customers, increased profits, and competitive advantage.

INDEX

A

Access to DM, as key success factor, 33
Account objectives, in selling process, 39
Account qualification; *see* Qualifying process
Account team, 37-39
Achievement phase of transition, 70-71, 99-121; *see also* People, development of; Processes, development of; Products, development of
Action steps, in selling process, 40-41
Activity time, 102
Adjusting, in selling process, 36
Affinity process, 13 n
Amplifying the voice of the customer (VOC), 74-81
  extended example, 78-81
  information obtained, 74-75
  research techniques, 74-75
  steps of, 75-78
    analyze, 77
    communicate, 77
    interview, 76-77
    select key accounts, 75-76
    transcribe, 77
Analysis; *see also* Force field analysis; Stakeholder analysis; Transition force field analysis
  amplifying the voice of the customer, 77
  performance data, 13-14
  qualifying process research, 33
  star performers, 83, 114-16
Assessment worksheet, for qualifying suspects, 34
Audits, as feedback, 54

B

Blueprinting; *see also* Critical tasks
  benefits of, 93-97
  blueprint, requirements and parts, 89-93
  focus, 91-93
  fundamental values, 90
  goals, 91
  vision, 90-91
  guidelines, 87-89
  outcomes of, 98
  rationale for, 85-87
  risks and opportunities, management of, 98
  as transition phase, 70, 85-98
Brache, A. P., 17 n, 25 n, 50 n
Brogowicz, A., 17 n
Business acumen, as critical capability, 49
Business fit, as key success factor, 33
Business impactors
  of expectations hierarchy, 5, 6
  Professional Services strategy and, 10-12
Business issues, assessment of
  example, 83-84
  outside experts, 82-83
  senior management interviews, 82
  steps of, 81-83
  strategic document review, 81-82

C

Category weighing techniques, 113 n
Change, resistance to, 60-61
  customers and, 65
Clark, K. B., 113 n

Clients
   conversion from customers, 41-42
   feedback from, 53
Coach role, of stakeholder, 124-26
Communication, stakeholder analysis
   and, 127
Competency
   competency profile, 117-18
   core competency and the blueprint,
     91-93
Competition, as key success factor, 33
Compliant personality type, of stake-
   holder, 125, 126
Consensus, democratic decisions ver-
   sus, 86 n
Consequences, establishment of, 53
Considerations, in selling process, 39
Consulting attitude, as key success factor, 33
Consulting process
   customers converted to clients, 41-42
   key consulting activities, 42
Contingency planning; see Opportunities; Risks
Core competency focus and, 91-93
Core processes, 25
   defining the processes, 27-43
Costs, must be quantified and
   managed, 111
Credibility, as key success factor, 33
Critical capabilities of teams, 11-12,
   47-49
   business acumen, 49
   project management, 48
   selling skills, 47-48
   technical knowledge, 48
Critical events, in selling process, 39
Critical tasks; see also People, development of; Processes, development
   of; Products, development of
   blueprint and, 96-97
   relationships, management of, 36, 96,
     123-27
Customer(s); see also Amplifying the
   voice of the customer (VOC)
   categorization of, 12-13

Customer(s) — *Cont.*
   converted to clients, 41-42
   customer value, maximization of,
     100
   defines value, 25, 111
   differences, 4-7
   exceeding customer expectations, 31
   expectation hierarchy, 5-6
   from prospects, 35
   resistance to change, 65
Cycle time, 102

D

Day-to-day tracking, 129-30
Deciding, in qualifying process, 33
Decision maker role, of stakeholder,
   124-25
Deming, W. E., 50 n
Discovery; see also Amplifying the
   voice of the customer; Business
   issues, assessment of
   analyzing star field performers, 83,
     114-16
   outcomes of, 84
   purposes of, 72
   traditional market research versus,
     73
   as transition phase, 69-70, 72-84
   as transition research, 72
Document review, as discovery step,
   81-82
Dominant personality type, of stakeholder, 125, 126
Drucker, Peter F., 49

E

EDS, 23
Eureka, William, 36 n
Expectation hierarchy (of customers),
   5-6
   business impactors, 5, 6
   givens, 5, 6
   wants, 5, 6

F

Facilitator, for blueprint sessions, 88
Feedback
    audits as, 54
    from clients, 53
    in performance system, 53-54
    requirements of, 53
Flexible structure, 22-23
Fluid information, 20-21
Focus, 4
    confirmation of business focus, 14
    core competency and, 91-93
    section of blueprint, 91-93
Focused power, 21-22
Focus groups, as research technique,
    74-75
Force field analysis; see Transition force
    field analysis
Four Ps, 17
Functional silos, 17-20
    typical marketing function, 17-18
    typical sales function, 18-19
    typical service function, 19
Fundamental values, 23-24
    section of blueprint, 90
Funding, as key success factor, 33

G

Gale, G. T., 111 n
Geier, J., 126 n
Givens, of expectations hierarchy, 5, 6
Goals
    performance goals, 100-101
    section of blueprint, 91
Gronroos, Christian, 9 n

H

Hanan, M., 30 n
Harrington, H. J., 25 n, 102 n
Hart, C. W. L., 113 n
Havel, G., 92 n
Heskett, J. L., 23 n, 113 n
High-impact training, 119-20

Hiring, outsourcing or training versus,
    49, 117

I

Impact Group, 5, 6 n, 10 n, 111 n
Implementer role, of stakeholder,
    124-25
Implementing
    in consulting process, 42
    new process, 107-8
    in selling process, 33
Importance to account, as key success
    factor, 33
Influencer personality type, of stake-
    holder, 125, 126
Influencer role, of stakeholder, 124-25
Information; see also Knowledge
    fluid information, 20-21
Innovating, in consulting process, 42
Interviews
    as research technique, 74-75
    senior management interviews, 82
ISO 9000
    certification, 54
    quality standards, 26

K

Kanter, R. M., 21 n
Key accounts, selection of, 75-76
Key success factors
    assessment worksheet, 34
    assessment worksheet, as force field
        analysis, 62
    in qualifying suspects, 32-34
Knowledge
    as power, 72
    as product, 11
    technical knowledge as critical, 48
Kotter, J. P., 23 n
Kuhlken, L. E., 51 n

L

Leads, 29

M

McCarthy, E. J., 17 n
McKinsey (firm), 23
Manuals, requirements of, 8
Marketing
    blueprint and, 94
    key activities of, 29
    leads converted to suspects, 29
    marketing process, 27-31
    promoting, 31
    research, 29
    testing, 31
    traditional prospecting does not
        work, 31
    typical marketing function, 17-18
Minimization (of performance level),
    92
Mizuno, S., 13 n

N

Networking, as promotion activity, 31

O

Off-the-shelf training, 119 n
Opportunities
    management of, 98, 127-29
    in selling process, 39
Organizing the business, 16-26
    flexible structure and, 22-23
    fluid information and, 20-21
    focused power and, 21-22
    functional silos, 17-20
    fundamental values, 23-24
    organizing around processes, 25-26
    principles of organizing, 20-25
Outsourcing
    hiring or training versus, 49, 117
    as product, 110
    in selling process, 38-39
Ownership, of processes, 101

P

Pay for performance pricing, 113

People, critical capabilities of, 11-12
People, development of, 97-98, 114-20
    analyze star performers, 83, 114-16
    compare current/required capabili-
        ties, 117
    competency profile, 117-18
    continuous learning, 120
    data analysis, 116-17
    high-impact training, 119-20
    hire/train/outsource, 117
    implement, 117
Performance data, analyzing the data,
    13-14
Performance system, 49-56
    consequences, establishment of, 53
    feedback, 53-54
    performance checklist, 54-55
    performance specifications, 50-52
    performance specifications, require-
        ments of, 51
    recognize and reward, 54
    resources, providing, 52-53
    work flow, determination of, 52
Personal and business issues, of stake-
    holders, 124, 125, 126
Personal fit, as key success factor, 34
Personality types, of stakeholders, 124,
    125, 126
Personnel; see People entries
Peters, T., 23 n, 30
Planning
    in consulting process, 42
    in selling process, 34-40
Porter, M. E., 6 n
Power
    focused power, 21-22
    knowledge as, 72
Prahalad, C. K., 92 n
Price; see also Pricing issues of Profes-
    sional Services
    pricing formula, 17, 112
    product development and, 97
    realistic pricing, 6
Pricing issues of Professional Services,
    110-14
    pricing maxims, 111-12

Pricing issues of Professional Services
— *Cont.*
pricing strategies, 112-14
pay for performance, 113
product design, 113-14
project, 112-13
time and materials, 112
Process engineering, as product, 110
Processes; *see also* Processes, development of; *and named processes*
blueprint and, 96
consulting process, 41-42
core processes, 25, 27, 28
defining the processes, 27-43
marketing process, 27-31
organizing around, 25-26
qualifying process, 32-34
selling process, 34-41
special challenges of, 42-43
support processes, 25
Processes, development of, 96, 100-108
action steps for, 101-8
create new process, 106-7
envision ideal process, 101-3
implement, 107-8
map existing process, 102-6
effective processes, 100-101
customer value, 100
ownership, 101
performance goals, 100-101
procedures, 101
simplicity, 101
Product(s); *see also* Products, development of
knowledge as, 11
pricing and product development, 97
product design pricing, 113-14
Products, development of, 97, 108-14;
see also Pricing issues of Professional Services
outsourcing, as product, 110
process engineering, as product, 110
training, as product, 109-10
Professional Services; *see also* Professional Services strategy

Professional Services — *Cont.*
business impactor customers and, 10-12
Professional Services strategy, 10-12
goal of, 11
selecting the strategy, 3-15
steps of selection process, 12-15
Project, as pricing strategy, 112-13
Project management, as critical capability, 48
Project manager, 42
Promoting
exceeding customer expectations, 31
in marketing process, 31
word-of-mouth activities, 30-31
Prospecting, traditional prospecting does not work, 31
Prospects, 32
converted to customers, 35
from suspects, 32
Publishing, as promotion activity, 31

Q

Qualifying process, 32-34
analyzing the research, 33
assessment worksheet, 34
blueprint and, 93-94
existing process, mapping of, 103-6
ideal process, 102-3
key success factors and, 32-34
research, 33
suspects converted to prospects, 34
Quality
quality function deployment (QFD), 13 n, 113 n
total quality management (TQM), 48
Quinn, J. B., 4 n, 23 n, 94 n

R

Realistic pricing, 6
Recruitment; *see also* Hiring
blueprint and, 93

Relationships
    management of, 96, 123-27
    relationship manager, 36
Research; *see also* Discovery
    in marketing process, 29
    in qualifying process, 33
    techniques, 74-75
    traditional market research, 72-74
Resources
    provision of, 52-53
    resource allocation, 6
    transition and, 66-67
Reward and recognize, 54
Risks
    management of, 98, 127-29
    in selling process, 39
Roles
    role shift to Professional Services,
        46-47
    of stakeholders, 124-26
Rummler, G. A., 17 n, 25 n, 50 n
Ryan, Nancy, 36 n

S

Sales; *see* Selling *entries*
Sasser, W. E., 113 n
Schein, E., 17 n
Selling; *see also* Selling process
    good old days of, 45-46
    role shift to Professional Services,
        46-47
    skill as critical capability, 47-48
    typical sales function, 18-19
Selling process, 34-41
    action steps, 40-41
    challenges of, 35
    key account planner, 37-38
    outsourcing, 38-39
    planning and, 34-40
    prospects converted to customers, 35
Service
    good old days of, 44-45
    role shift to Professional Services,
        46-47

Service — *Cont.*
    typical service function, 19
Shewhart cycle, 36 n
Simplicity, of processes, 101
Speaking, as promotion activity, 30-31
Stakeholder analysis
    blueprint and, 95-96
    communication and, 127
    relationship management and,
        124-26
    in selling process, 39
Stakeholder(s); *see also* Stakeholder
        analysis
    buy in, of blueprint, 93
    buy in, of implementation, 107-8
    defined, 95
    personal and business issues, 124,
        125, 126
    personality types, 124, 125, 126
    roles of, 124-26
Star performers, analysis of, 83, 114-16
Steady personality type, of stake-
        holder, 125, 126
Strategies, sales and service; *see also*
        Professional Services strategy
    traditional, 7-9
    value-added, 7, 9-10
Structure, flexible structure, 22-23
Support processes, 25
Suspects
    converted to prospects, 32
    from leads, 29

T

Teams; *see also* Critical capabilities of
        teams; Performance system
    building high-performance teams,
        44-56
    transition project team, 68-69
Technical knowledge, as critical capa-
        bility, 48
Testing, in marketing process, 31
Time and materials, as pricing strategy,
        112

Timing, as key success factor, 33
Total quality management (TQM), 48
Tracking
   activities included, 130
   in consulting process, 42
   day-to-day tracking, 129-30
   manage relationships, 123-27
   manage risks and opportunities,
      127-29
   in selling process, 36
   as transition phase, 71, 122-30
Training
   high-impact training, 119-20
   off-the-shelf training, 119 n
   outsourcing or hiring versus, 49, 117
   as product, 109-10
Transition; *see also* Transition, phases
      of; Transition force field analysis;
   managing the, 59-71
   resistance to change, 60-61
   transition project, 67-68
   transition project plan, 94-95
   transition project team, 68-69
Transition, phases of, 69-71; *see also*
      entries for named phases
   achievement, 70-71
   blueprinting, 70, 85-98
   discovery, 69-70, 72-84
   tracking, 71
Transition force field analysis, 61-67
   blueprint and, 96
   customer value, 65
   key success factor assessment as, 62
   leadership and, 65-66
   resources and, 66-67

Transition force field analysis — *Cont.*
   senior management commitment,
      62-64
   steps to, 62

V

Value; *see also* Values
   customer defines, 25, 111
   customer value, maximization of,
      100
   should be quantified, 111
   value-to-price ratio, 111
Value-added strategy, 7, 9-10
Value Leadership Benchmarking, 111 n
Values; *see also* Value
   fundamental values, 23-24, 90
   section of blueprint, 90
Vision, section of blueprint, 90-91
VOC; *see* Amplifying the voice of the
      customer

W

Wants, of expectations hierarchy, 5, 6
Waste, contributions to, 25-26
Weisbord, M., 87 n
Wheelwright, S. C., 113 n
Word-of-mouth promotion activities,
      30-31
   networking, 31
   publishing, 31
   speaking, 30-31
Work flow, determination of, 52